Target
Get back on track

3

E

Edexcel GCSE (9–1)
English Language
Reading

David Grant

Published by Pearson Education Limited, 80 Strand, London, WC2R ORL.

www.pearsonschoolsandfecolleges.co.uk

Text © Pearson Education Limited 2017
Produced and typeset by Tech-Set Ltd, Gateshead

The right of David Grant to be identified as author of this work has been asserted by him in accordance with the Copyright, Designs and Patents Act 1988.

First published 2017

20 19 18 17
10 9 8 7 6 5 4 3 2 1

British Library Cataloguing in Publication Data
A catalogue record for this book is available from the British Library

ISBN 978 0435 18325 7

Printed in Slovakia by Neografia

We are grateful to the following for permission to reproduce copyright material:

Text 1 on page 2 from *Fast Food Nation: What The All-American Meal is Doing to the World*, Penguin (Eric Schlosser) pp.19-20, FAST FOOD NATION by Eric Schlosser (Penguin Books Ltd, 2001) Copyright © Eric Schlosser, 2001. Reproduced by permission of Penguin Books Ltd; **Text 1 on page 18** from *The Life of Ian Fleming* 1st ed., Bloomsbury Academic (John Pearson 2013) pp.266-268, Extract from The Life of Ian Fleming by John Pearson reprinted by permission of Peters Fraser & Dunlop (www.petersfraserdunlop.com) on behalf of John Pearson; **Text 1 on page 26** from *Of Men and Their Making: The Harvest Gypsies: Squatter's Camps* Penguin Classics (John Steinbeck) pp.78-79; **Text 1 on page 34** from Experience: I fell out of the sky, *Guardian* (Matthew Blake; Neil Laughton), https://www.theguardian.com/lifeandstyle/2014/may/09/experience-i-fell-out-of-the-sky, Copyright Guardian News & Media Ltd 2016; **Text 1 on page 50** from *Let Us Now Praise Famous Men: Three Tenant Families'* 1st Mariner Books Ed Houghton Mifflin (Trade) (James Agee and Walker Evans) 374, Excerpt from LET US NOW PRAISE FAMOUS MEN. Copyright ©, 1939, 1940 by James Agee. Copyright ©, 1941 by James Agee and Walker Evans. Copyright © renewed 1969 by Mia Fritsch Agee and Walker Evans. Used by permission of Houghton Mifflin Co. All rights reserved.; **Text 2 on page 50** from *The Life And Times of the Thunderbolt Kid: Travels Through my Childhood*, Black Swan (Bill Bryson 2015) pp.262-263, Excerpt(s) from THE LIFE AND TIMES OF THE THUNDERBOLT KID: A MEMOIR by Bill Bryson, copyright © 2006 by Bill Bryson. Used by permission of Broadway Books, an imprint of the Crown Publishing Group, a division of Penguin Random House LLC. All rights reserved. and Reprinted with permission of Bill Bryson; **Text 1 on page 58** from *Never Cry Wolf: Amazing True Story of Life Among Arctic Wolves* Penguin Modern Classics Edition, McClelland & Stewart (Farley Mowat 2009) p.161; **Text 2 on page 58** from Pet tales: Poppy, retired racing greyhound, *The Telegraph* 08/08/2012 (Rachel Hawkins), © Telegraph Media Group Limited 2012; **More Practice Text 3** from *Going Commando* John Blake Publishing Ltd (Mark Time 2015), From Going Commando by Mark Time, Published by John Blake Publishing

Contents

This workbook has been developed using the Pearson Progression Map and Scale for English.

To find out more about the Progression Scale for English and to see how it relates to indicative GCSE 9–1 grades go to www.pearsonschools.co.uk/ProgressionServices

Helping you to formulate grade predictions, apply interventions and track progress.

Any reference to indicative grades in the Pearson Target Workbooks and Pearson Progression Services is not to be used as an accurate indicator of how a student will be awarded a grade for their GCSE exams.

You have told us that mapping the Steps from the Pearson Progression Maps to indicative grades will make it simpler for you to accumulate the evidence to formulate your own grade predictions, apply any interventions and track student progress. We're really excited about this work and its potential for helping teachers and students. It is, however, important to understand that this mapping is for guidance only to support teachers' own predictions of progress and is not an accurate predictor of grades.

Our Pearson Progression Scale is criterion referenced. If a student can perform a task or demonstrate a skill, we say they are working at a certain Step according to the criteria. Teachers can mark assessments and issue results with reference to these criteria which do not depend on the wider cohort in any given year. For GCSE exams however, all Awarding Organisations set the grade boundaries with reference to the strength of the cohort in any given year. For more information about how this works please visit: https://qualifications.pearson.com/en/support/support-topics/results-certification/understanding-marks-and-grades.html/Teacher

The activities in this workbook have been developed to support students in attaining the 5th, 6th and 7th Steps in the Progression Scale, focusing on those barriers to progression identified in the Pearson Progression Scale.

5th Step	6th Step	7th Step
A growing range of **reading** strategies to tackle unfamiliar words. Attempts to summarise and synthesise **key points** from a text. Draws **inferences** from specific evidence. **Critical responses** are more analytical and formal, supported with straightforward comments on the writer's **whole text** and **language choices** and their impact on the reader.	Frequent monitoring of **reading** comprehension. Some effective summary and synthesis of **key points** from a text. Draws **inferences** from close reading. Increasingly competent **critical responses** consider the writer's **whole text** and **language choices**, making more detailed comments on their impact.	Monitors **reading** comprehension increasingly consistently. Summarises and synthesises a range of **key points** from a text with some skill. Draws securely founded **inferences** from close reading. **Critical responses** are more confident, beginning to focus on how the writer's **whole text** and **language choices** have shaped a text and the reader's response.

Unit title and skills boost	Pearson Progression Scale: Barriers (difficulties students may encounter when working towards this step)	Assessment Objectives	Texts used and paper covered
Unit 1 Tackling an unseen text **Skills boost 1** How do I identify the key ideas in the text? **Skills boost 2** How do I track the writer's purpose and intention? **Skills boost 3** How do I know I have understood the text?	• May make judgements that are not supported by a sufficient weight of evidence or that lack balance e.g. may be based on single points in a text or not take into account conflicting information. (Step 5) • May lack confidence or stamina for tracing the development of ideas in longer or more complex texts. (Step 6) • Challenge of simultaneously holding in mind the whole text and focusing in on specific details. (Step 7)	Identify and interpret explicit and implicit information and ideas (AO1)	*Fast Food Nation* by Eric Schlosser, 2001 Paper 2
Unit 2 Analysing a text **Skills boost 1** How do I begin to analyse a text? **Skills boost 2** How do I choose evidence? **Skills boost 3** How do I analyse a quotation?	• Can find it difficult to structure critical responses to texts… finds it hard to know which features to single out and prioritise. (Step 5) • Struggles to incorporate evidence into written response fluently, e.g. knowing how much to quote or how to embed quotation. (Step 6) • Explanations may paraphrase quotations and offer semantic explanations… especially when student is following a paragraph 'formula' such as PEE. (Step 7)	Select and synthesise evidence (AO1) Explain, comment on and analyse how writers use language and structure to achieve effects and influence readers (AO2)	*Tess of the D'Urbervilles* by Thomas Hardy, 1891 Paper 1
Unit 3 Commenting on language **Skills boost 1** How do I start to think about commenting on language? **Skills boost 2** How do I choose which language to write about? **Skills boost 3** How do I comment on the writer's use of language?	• May struggle to describe and explain writers' choices and their intended effects, especially in writing; comments may be too generalised and lack precision e.g. 'the adjectives are really descriptive'. (Step 5) • May take individual words or sentences out of context of the paragraph or whole text so that their meaning is distorted. (Step 6) • Overly focused on terminology. (Step 7)	Explain, comment on and analyse how writers use language and structure to achieve effects and influence readers (AO2)	*The Life of Ian Fleming* by John Pearson, 1966 Paper 2
Unit 4 Commenting on structure **Skills boost 1** How do I identify the effects of whole text structure? **Skills boost 2** How do I identify the effects of sentence structure choices? **Skills boost 3** How do I comment on the writer's use of structure?	• May not appreciate that writers deliberately organise and structure sentences to manipulate the reader's response. (Step 5) • May take individual words or sentences out of context of the paragraph or whole text so that their meaning is distorted. (Step 6) • May find it difficult to balance attention between reading holistically to link ideas, themes and intentions of the whole text, with a close focus on particular words or sentences. (Step 7)	Explain, comment on and analyse how writers use language and structure to achieve effects and influence readers (AO2)	*Death in the Dust* by John Steinbeck, 1936 Paper 2
Unit 5 Commenting on language and structure **Skills boost 1** How do I write about language and structure? **Skills boost 2** How do I choose the best evidence for commenting on language and structure? **Skills boost 3** How do I comment on language and structure?	• May not appreciate that writers deliberately organise and structure sentences to manipulate the reader's response. (Step 5) • May struggle to describe and explain writers' choices and their intended effects, especially in writing; comments may be too generalised and lack precision e.g. 'the adjectives are really descriptive'. (Step 5) • May take individual words or sentences out of context of the paragraph or whole text so that their meaning is distorted. (Step 6) • Overly focused on terminology. (Step 7)	Explain, comment on and analyse how writers use language and structure to achieve effects and influence readers (AO2)	*I Fell Out of the Sky* in the *Guardian*, 2014 Paper 2

Unit title and skills boost	Pearson Progression Scale: Barriers (difficulties students may encounter when working towards this step)	Assessment Objectives	Texts used and paper covered
Unit 6 Evaluating texts **Skills boost 1** How do I identify where the writer has tried to achieve their intention? **Skills boost 2** How do I comment on the writer's intention? **Skills boost 3** How do I evaluate the writer's success?	• Can find it difficult to structure critical responses to texts… finds it hard to know which features to single out and prioritise. (Step 5) • Struggles to incorporate evidence into written response fluently, e.g. knowing how much to quote or how to embed quotation. (Step 6) • Explanations may paraphrase quotations and offer semantic explanations… especially when student is following a paragraph 'formula' such as PEE. (Step 7)	Evaluate texts critically (AO4)	*Dracula* by Bram Stoker, 1897 Paper 1
Unit 7 Synthesising and comparing **Skills boost 1** How do I identify points of comparison? **Skills boost 2** How do I synthesise information and ideas in two texts? **Skills boost 3** How do I write a comparison?	• May struggle to locate specific examples to support points, especially in denser text or when comparing texts. (Step 5) • Can find it difficult to structure critical responses to texts, especially when comparisons are called for; finds it hard to know which features to single out and prioritise; likely to 'work through' a text, making comments as they go. (Step 5) • Use of reading skills may not be assured enough to deal with more complex information or to cross-reference between texts. (Step 6) • Comparisons may not be well balanced e.g. more attention is given to one text or comments may focus on a narrow range of features. (Step 7)	Select and synthesise evidence from different texts (AO1)	*Let Us Now Praise Famous Men* by James Agee and Walker Evans, 1941 and *The Life and Times of the Thunderbolt Kid* by Bill Bryson, 2006 Paper 1
Unit 8 Comparing ideas and perspectives **Skills boost 1** How do I identify relevant ideas and perspectives? **Skills boost 2** How do I compare ideas and perspectives? **Skills boost 3** How do I develop my comparison?	• Limited awareness of the different features of a text that can be compared. More likely to focus on content and ideas than features of style. (Step 4) • Can find it difficult to structure critical responses to texts, especially when comparisons are called for; finds it hard to know which features to single out and prioritise; likely to 'work through' a text, making comments as they go. (Step 5) • May struggle to locate specific examples. (Step 6) • Comments may focus on a narrow range of features. (Step 7)	Compare writers' ideas and perspectives, as well as how these are conveyed (AO3)	*Never Cry Wolf* by Farley Mowat, 1963 and Pet tales: Poppy, retired racing greyhound, in *The Telegraph*, 2012 Paper 2
Unit 9 Expressing your ideas clearly and precisely **Skills boost 1** How do I write a formal, analytical response? **Skills boost 2** How do I express my ideas precisely? **Skills boost 3** How do I express my ideas clearly?	• May not use appropriate technical or critical vocabulary when discussing the writer's style and techniques. (Step 6) • Understanding of what has been read may not be adequately demonstrated because students are struggling to write in a formal analytical style. (Step 8)	Identify and interpret explicit and implicit information and ideas (AO1)	*Oliver Twist* by Charles Dickens, 1837 Paper 1
More practice texts	Three additional extracts referenced in the additional exam-style question provided at the end of each unit.		*The Cold Hand* by Felix Octavius Carr Darley, 1846 *The Battle of the Somme* by Rif Baer, 1916 *Going Commando* by Mark Time, 2015

① Tackling an unseen text

This unit will help you tackle an unseen text. The skills you will build are to:

- identify key ideas in the text
- track how the writer's ideas develop in the text
- explore how the writer's ideas help to achieve their purpose and intention
- check your understanding of the text.

In the exam, you will face questions like the ones below. These are about the text on page 2. This unit will prepare you to write your own response to these questions.

Exam-style question

1 From lines 10–15, give **two** reasons why the McDonald brothers decided to close their drive-in restaurant. (2 marks)

2 From lines 1–9, give **one** example that suggests how much money the McDonald brothers made from their Burger Bar Drive-in. (1 mark)

The three key questions in the **skills boosts** will help you tackle an unseen text.

 1 How do I identify the key ideas in the text?

 2 How do I track the writer's purpose and intention?

 3 How do I know I have understood the text?

Read the extract on page 2 from *Fast Food Nation* by Eric Schlosser, published in 2001. You will tackle a 21st-century non-fiction extract in the Reading section of your Paper 2 exam.

As you read, remember the following: ⊘

Before reading the extract, carefully read any introduction provided. It is intended to help you understand where the text is taken from and other useful background information you might need.

While reading the extract, if you lose understanding of the text, stop and re-read from the last sentence or paragraph that you clearly understood.

After reading the extract, read it again.

In this extract, the writer explains how the founders of McDonald's restaurants changed the way that fast food was made and served.

Text 1 Fast Food Nation, Eric Schlosser

Richard and Maurice McDonald had left New Hampshire for southern California at the start of the Depression, hoping to find jobs in Hollywood. They worked as set builders on the Columbia Film Studios back lot, saved their money, and bought a movie theater in Glendale. The theater was not a success. In 1937 they opened a drive-in restaurant in Pasadena, trying to cash in on the new craze, hiring three **carhops** and selling mainly hot dogs. A
5   few years later they moved to a larger building on E Street in San Bernardino and opened the McDonald Brothers Burger Bar Drive-In. The new restaurant was located near a high school, employed twenty carhops, and promptly made the brothers rich. Richard and "Mac" McDonald bought one of the largest houses in San Bernardino, a hillside mansion with a tennis court and a pool.

By the end of the 1940s the McDonald brothers had grown dissatisfied with the drive-in business. They were tired
10   of constantly looking for new carhops and short-order cooks — who were in great demand — as the old ones left for higher-paying jobs elsewhere. They were tired of replacing the dishes, glassware, and silverware their teenage customers constantly broke or ripped off. And they were tired of their teenage customers. The brothers thought about selling the restaurant. Instead, they tried something new.

The McDonalds fired all their carhops in 1948, closed their restaurant, installed larger grills, and reopened three
15   months later with a radically new method of preparing food. It was designed to increase the speed, lower prices, and raise the volume of sales. The brothers eliminated almost two-thirds of the items on their old menu. They got rid of everything that had to be eaten with a knife, spoon, or fork. The only sandwiches now sold were hamburgers or cheeseburgers. The brothers got rid of their dishes and glassware, replacing them with paper cups, paper bags, and paper plates. They divided the food preparation into separate tasks performed by different workers. To fill
20   a typical order, one person grilled the hamburger; another "dressed" and wrapped it; another prepared the milk shake; another made the fries; and another worked the counter. For the first time, the guiding principles of a factory assembly line were applied to a commercial kitchen. The new division of labor meant that a worker only had to be taught how to perform one task. Skilled and expensive short-order cooks were no longer necessary. All of the burgers were sold with the same condiments: ketchup, onions, mustard, and two pickles. No substitutions
25   were allowed. The McDonald brothers' Speedee Service System revolutionized the restaurant business. An ad of theirs seeking **franchisees** later spelled out the benefits of the system: "Imagine — No Carhops — No Waitresses — No Dishwashers — No BusBoys — The McDonald's System is Self-Service!"

The Speedee Service System, however, got off to a rocky start. Customers pulled up to the restaurant and honked their horns, wondering what had happened to the carhops, still expecting to be served. People were not yet
30   accustomed to waiting in line and getting their own food. Within a few weeks, however, the new system gained acceptance, as word spread about the low prices and good hamburgers. The McDonald brothers now aimed for a much broader clientele. They employed only young men, convinced that female workers would attract teenage boys to the restaurant and drive away other customers. Families soon lined up to eat at McDonald's. Company historian John F. Love explained the lasting significance of McDonald's new self-service system: "Working-class
35   families could finally afford to feed their kids restaurant food."

carhops: waiters who serve food to customers in their cars at a drive-in restaurant

franchisees: the owner of a business who has bought the right to use the name and sell the products of an established business. More than half of McDonald's restaurants in the UK are owned and run by franchisees.

1 How do I identify the key ideas in the text?

When you first read an unseen text, you need to identify the key ideas and information in each section of the text.

① Read the first paragraph of the extract on page 2.

Look at some ideas and information that the writer has included.

A.	The McDonald brothers bought a cinema but it was not successful.	
B.	The McDonald brothers ran a very successful drive-in restaurant business.	
C.	The McDonald brothers' first restaurant sold mainly hot dogs.	
D.	Richard McDonald was a very experienced chef.	
E.	The McDonald brothers came from New Hampshire.	

Label ✏ each piece of information above to identify whether you think it is:

• the key idea of the first paragraph, write ✏ **KEY**

• additional detail, write ✏ **DETAIL**

• not included in the first paragraph, mark with a ⊗.

② Now look at the rest of the extract.

ⓐ Write ✏ **one** sentence summarising the main idea in each section.

Paragraph 2: ....

....

.... ☐

....

Paragraph 3: ....

....

.... ☐

....

Paragraph 4: ....

....

.... ☐

....

ⓑ Now check your answers to question ② ⓐ to make sure you have:

• focused on the main idea in each paragraph

• not focused on additional details which are less important than the main idea.

Tick ✓ any that you are happy with and change ✏ any that you are not happy with.

2 How do I track the writer's purpose and intention?

Every text has:
- **a purpose**: the reason it was written, for example, to give information or to explain how to do something
- **an intention**: the impact that the writer intends the text to have on the reader, for example, to interest the reader or to change their opinion.

Identifying and tracking the **purpose** and **intention** of an unseen text is a very effective way to develop your understanding of it.

① **a** Which of these **purposes** does the extract on page 2 have? Tick ✓ at least **one**.

argue
☐ to express the writer's opinion on a topic and influence the reader's opinion

persuade
☐ to influence the reader's actions or decisions

inform
☐ to give the reader information

explain
☐ to tell the reader how to do something or how something happened

describe
☐ to create a clear impression of a person, event or situation

b Find **one** section or sentence in the text where the writer has achieved **each** purpose you have ticked. Underline Ⓐ and label 🖉 it/them.

② Now think about the writer's intention in the extract on page 2.

a What impressions, thoughts or feelings does the writer want the reader to have when they read about the McDonald brothers? Tick ✓ any of the impressions below that you were given by the extract.

  i. The McDonald brothers were very lucky businessmen.

A.
☐

  ii. The McDonald brothers were very clever businessmen.

B.
☐

  iii. The McDonald brothers were very ruthless businessmen.

C.
☐

b Find **one** section or sentence in the text where the writer created **each** impression you have ticked. Circle Ⓐ and label 🖉 it/them.

c Write 🖉 **one** sentence summing up the impression that the writer of the extract has given you of the way the McDonald brothers ran their restaurant.

....

....

....

4   Unit 1 Tackling an unseen text

3 How do I know I have understood the text?

One way to check your understanding of a text is to try to sum up its main ideas and the impression it creates in just one sentence.

1 Look at some students' summaries of the text on page 2.

a Which one most accurately sums up the main ideas in the text? Tick ✓ it.

Student A | It's about McDonald's restaurants. | ☐

Student B | The McDonald brothers were very clever businessmen. | ☐

Student C | McDonald's started selling burgers a very long time ago. | ☐

Student D | The McDonald brothers invented the way that fast food is made and sold. | ☐

b Write ✐ just **one** sentence summing up **your understanding** of the key ideas, and the impressions created, in the text.

....

....

....

....

....

c Look again at the extract on page 2, thinking about the main idea in each paragraph. Does your summary of the whole text include all of those main ideas? If not, change ✐ your answer to question **1** **b** to make sure it does.

2 Finally, think about how your impressions changed as you read the extract on page 2. Complete ✐ these sentences.

In the first paragraph, I got the impression that ....

....

....

When I had finished reading the text, I was left with the impression that ....

....

....

....

Tackling an unseen text

When you tackle an unseen text, aim to:

- read the text very carefully.
- identify the key ideas and information in each paragraph or section of the text.
- think about the writer's purpose and intention: what impressions does the text create?
- check your understanding of the text by summing up its key ideas and information and the impression it creates.
- think about how your impressions change as you read the text; when you have finished reading the text, are your impressions the same as they were when you started reading?

Some of the questions you will face in your exams are designed to test your skill in extracting information from an unseen text. Once you have read and understood the text fully, you are ready to tackle these kinds of question.

Now look at one student's answer to the exam-style questions below, which refer to the text on page 2.

Exam-style question

1 From lines 32–40, give **one** reason why the McDonald brothers' restaurant was popular with families.   **(1 mark)**

   Working class families could afford it.

2 From lines 16–31, give **two** examples that suggest how much the McDonald brothers changed the way they ran their restaurant.   **(2 marks)**

   1 *They got rid of everything on the menu that had to be eaten with a knife, spoon, or fork.*

   2 *It says that they 'revolutionized the restaurant business'.*

(1) Which of this student's answers are correct? Tick ✓ them.

(2) Which of this student's answers are incorrect? Cross them ✗ and write ✏ your own correct answers below.

....

....

Your turn!

After you have read and understood the text, identified its key ideas and the impressions it creates, you are ready to tackle **all of the questions** you are likely to be asked in your exam.

Test your understanding by completing 🖉 the exam-style question below.

Richard and Maurice McDonald had left New Hampshire for southern California at the start of the Depression, hoping to find jobs in Hollywood. They worked as set builders on the Columbia Film Studios back lot, saved their money, and bought a movie theater in Glendale. The theater was not a success. In 1937 they opened a drive-in restaurant in Pasadena, trying to cash in on the new craze, hiring three **carhops** and selling mainly hot dogs. A
5 few years later they moved to a larger building on E Street in San Bernardino and opened the McDonald Brothers Burger Bar Drive-In. The new restaurant was located near a high school, employed twenty carhops, and promptly made the brothers rich. Richard and "Mac" McDonald bought one of the largest houses in San Bernardino, a hillside mansion with a tennis court and a pool.

By the end of the 1940s the McDonald brothers had grown dissatisfied with the drive-in business. They were tired
10 of constantly looking for new carhops and short-order cooks — who were in great demand — as the old ones left for higher-paying jobs elsewhere. They were tired of replacing the dishes, glassware, and silverware their teenage customers constantly broke or ripped off. And they were tired of their teenage customers. The brothers thought about selling the restaurant. Instead, they tried something new.

Exam-style question

1 From lines 1–8, give **one** example that suggests how much money the McDonald brothers made from their Burger Bar Drive-In. **(1 mark)**

....

....

....

....

2 From lines 9–13, give **two** reasons why the McDonald brothers decided to close their drive-in restaurant. **(2 marks)**

1 ....

....

2 ....

....

Review your skills

Check up

Review your response to the exam-style question on page 7 and your understanding of the text on page 2. Tick ⊘ the column to show how well you think you have done each of the following.

	Not quite ⊘	Nearly there ⊘	Got it! ⊘
identified key ideas and information in the text	☐	☐	☐
identified the writer's purpose and intention and the impressions the text creates	☐	☐	☐
understood the text	☐	☐	☐

Need more practice?

Below is another exam-style question, this time relating to text 2 on page 74: *The Battle of the Somme* by Rif Baer. You'll find some suggested points to refer to in the Answers section.

Before you tackle the question:

- read the text carefully
- identify the main ideas or information in the text
- think about the purpose of the text and the writer's intentions: what impressions do you get from the text? Do they change as you read it?
- sum up the main ideas in the text and the impressions it creates.

Exam-style question

1 From lines 1–5, give **one** reason why the general offensive will begin without the writer and his comrades. **(1 mark)**

....

2 From lines 6–8, give **two** examples that suggest the hustle and bustle. **(2 marks)**

1 ....

....

2 ....

....

How confident do you feel about each of these **skills?** Colour ✎ in the bars.

① How do I identify the key ideas in the text? ☐☐☐☐

② How do I track the writer's purpose and intention? ☐☐☐☐

③ How do I know I have understood the text? ☐☐☐☐

Get started

Select and synthesise evidence (AO1)
Explain, comment on and analyse how writers use language
and structure to achieve effects and influence readers (AO2)

② Analysing a text

This unit will help you analyse a text. The skills you will build are to:

- identify relevant ideas to explore in your analysis
- choose relevant evidence from the text to support ideas
- analyse the writer's choices in the evidence you select.

In the exam, you will face questions like the one below. This is about the text on page 10.
This unit will prepare you to write your own response to this question.

The three key questions in the **skills boosts** will help you analyse the text.

 How do I begin to analyse a text?

 How do I choose evidence?

 How do I analyse a quotation?

Read the extract on page 10 from *Tess of the D'Urbervilles* by Thomas Hardy, first published in 1891.
You will tackle a 19th-century fiction extract in the Reading section of your Paper 1 exam.

As you read, remember the following:

Check you understand the focus of the exam-style question you are preparing to respond to.

Think about the ways in which the writer shows what has happened in the upstairs room.

Mark or underline any parts of the text which you could use in your response to the question.

Mrs Brooks has rented a room to Mr and Mrs D'Urberville. When she hears them arguing, she becomes interested and listens carefully.

Text 1 Tess of the D'Urbervilles, Thomas Hardy

Overhead, as she sat, she could now hear the floorboards slightly creak, as if some one were walking about, and presently the movement was explained by the rustle of garments against the banisters, the opening and the closing of the front door, and the form of Tess passing to the gate on her way into the street. She was fully dressed now in the walking costume of a well-to-do young lady in which she had arrived, with the sole addition that over
5   her hat and black feathers a veil was drawn.

Mrs Brooks had not been able to catch any word of farewell, temporary or otherwise, between her tenants at the door above. They might have quarrelled, or Mr d'Urberville might still be asleep, for he was not an early riser.

She went into the back room, which was more especially her own apartment, and continued her sewing there. The lady lodger did not return, nor did the gentleman ring his bell. Mrs Brooks pondered on the delay, and on what
10   probable relation the visitor who had called so early bore to the couple upstairs. In reflecting she leant back in her chair.

As she did so her eyes glanced casually over the ceiling till they were arrested by a spot in the middle of its white surface which she had never noticed there before. It was about the size of a wafer when she first observed it, but it speedily grew as large as the palm of her hand, and then she could perceive that it was red. The oblong white
15   ceiling, with this scarlet blot in the midst, had the appearance of a gigantic ace of hearts.

Mrs Brooks had strange qualms of misgiving. She got upon the table, and touched the spot in the ceiling with her fingers. It was damp, and she fancied that it was a blood stain.

Descending from the table, she left the parlour, and went upstairs, intending to enter the room overhead, which was the bedchamber at the back of the drawing-room. But, **nerveless** woman as she had now become, she could
20   not bring herself to attempt the handle. She listened. The dead silence within was broken only by a regular beat.

Drip, drip, drip.

Mrs Brooks hastened downstairs, opened the front door, and ran into the street. A man she knew, one of the workmen employed at an adjoining villa, was passing by, and she begged him to come in and go upstairs with her; she feared something had happened to one of her lodgers. The workman **assented**, and followed her to
25   the landing.

She opened the door of the drawing-room, and stood back for him to pass in, entering herself behind him. The room was empty; the breakfast—a substantial **repast** of coffee, eggs, and a cold ham—lay spread upon the table untouched, as when she had taken it up, excepting that the carving-knife was missing. She asked the man to go through the folding-doors into the adjoining room.

30   He opened the doors, entered a step or two, and came back almost instantly with a rigid face. "My good God, the gentleman in bed is dead! I think he has been hurt with a knife—a lot of blood had run down upon the floor!"

nerveless: unafraid
assented: agreed
repast: meal

How do I begin to analyse a text?

To begin your analysis, you need to:
- make sure you know what the question is asking you to analyse
- identify relevant ideas you can use in your response to the question.

(1) Read the exam-style question again.

Exam-style question

In lines 12–21, how does the writer use language and structure to show what has happened in the upstairs room?

Support your views with reference to the text.   **(6 marks)**

Now look at the first three sentences of the part of the text on page 10 that the question asks you to focus on.

A.

As she did so her eyes glanced casually over the ceiling till they were arrested by a spot in the middle of its white surface which she had never noticed there before.

B.

It was about the size of a wafer when she first observed it, but it speedily grew as large as the palm of her hand, and then she perceive that it was red.

C.

The oblong white ceiling, with this scarlet blot in the midst, had the appearance of a gigantic ace of hearts.

(a) Cross (X) any of the sentences above that are not relevant to the question you are answering.

(b) Which one of the sentences above do you think is most interesting or effective? Tick (✓) it.

You might choose it because you feel the writer has:
- described something particularly vividly
- shown a character's thoughts and feelings very clearly
- made you react strongly to the ideas or events in the text.

Alternatively, there might be another reason why you find it interesting or effective.

(c) Write ✐ one sentence explaining your choice.

....

....

....

....

....

(d) Look again at the rest of the text you are being asked to focus on in this question.

Choose **two** more sentences that you feel are **the most** interesting or effective.
Label ✐ them 'A' and 'B' and add ✐ a note to each one explaining your choice.

How do I choose evidence?

When you analyse a text, you need to support your ideas with evidence from the text. Aim to choose short, relevant quotations that will help you answer the question you are responding to.

① Read again the exam-style question from page 9.

Exam-style question

In lines 12–21, how does the writer use language and structure to show what has happened in the upstairs room?

Support your views with reference to the text.

(6 marks)

Now look at one student's response to this question.

> The writer clearly describes the blood stain on the ceiling so you can see how big and red it is. 'The oblong white ceiling, with this scarlet blot in the midst, had the appearance of a gigantic ace of hearts.'

a Which are the most interesting and effective words or phrases in the quotation they use? Circle Ⓐ them.

b Which parts of this evidence could you cut to leave a relevant, focused, short quotation? Draw a line 🖉 through all the parts of the quotation that are not needed.

② Look at this exam-style question.

Exam style question

From lines 16–20, give **two** ways in which the writer shows that Mrs Brooks is worried. You may use your own words or quotations from the text.

a Underline Ⓐ **two** sentences in the extract below which you could use to answer the question.

> Mrs Brooks had strange qualms of misgiving. She got upon the table, and touched the spot in the ceiling with her fingers. It was damp, and she fancied that it was a blood stain.
>
> Descending from the table, she left the parlour, and went upstairs, intending to enter the room overhead, which was the bedchamber at the back of the drawing-room. But, **nerveless** woman as she had now become, she could
> 20 not bring herself to attempt the handle. She listened. The dead silence within was broken only by a regular beat.

b Do you need to use the whole of each of your chosen sentences to answer the question? Or could you just use the most important, relevant part of each sentence? Write 🖉 your answer to the above question in the space below.

....

....

....

3 **How do I analyse a quotation?**

When you analyse a quotation, you need to think about the **effect** of the writer's choices in the quotation and their **impact** on the reader.

1. Look at the first part of a student's paragraph written in response to a question about the writer's use of language in the extract on page 10.

> The writer clearly describes the blood stain on the ceiling so you can see how big and red it is: 'the appearance of a gigantic ace of hearts'.

Which of the three pieces of analysis below would make the most effective comment to finish off the paragraph above? Draw (✏) lines linking the notes on the right to the analysis on the left.

A.
> Describing it as 'gigantic' makes it seem really huge as though it is getting bigger and bigger.

Least effective:
Simply repeats the main point of the paragraph.

B.
> Comparing it to the ace of hearts makes you think of hearts and blood which makes it more worrying.

More effective:
Comments on the effect of the writer's choices in the quotation.

C.
> Describing it in this way makes you see how big and red it is.

Most effective:
Comments on the effect of the writer's choices in the quotation **and** their impact on the reader.

2. Look at a student's notes on one part of the extract on page 10.

short sentence makes it stand out

scary sound of blood dripping

> She listened. The dead silence within was broken only by a regular beat. Drip, drip, drip..

you can imagine blood hitting the floor

repeating the word adds tension and drama

Use the student's notes and your own ideas to complete (✏) their paragraph of analysis below. Aim to comment on the effect of the writer's choices and/or their impact on the reader.

> The writer describes the sound of blood dripping from the murdered man: 'Drip, drip, drip'.

....

....

....

Analysing a text

To write a good analysis, you need to:

- make sure you know what the question is asking you to do
- identify relevant ideas in the text that will help you answer the question
- select short, relevant quotations to support those ideas
- analyse the writer's choices in those quotations, commenting on their effect and/or their impact on the reader.

Now look at this exam-style question, which you saw at the start of the unit.

Exam-style question

In lines 12–21, how does the writer use language and structure to show what has happened in the upstairs room?

Support your views with reference to the text.

(6 marks)

(1) Look at this paragraph from one student's response to the exam-style question above. Link ✎ the annotations to the paragraph, to show where the student has used each element of a successful paragraph of analysis.

| identifies a relevant idea from the text |

The writer describes how Mrs Brooks tries to work out what the stain on the ceiling is: 'touched the spot on the ceiling with her fingers. It was damp'. This shows she is trying to work out what the stain is. The writer says she touched it 'with her fingers' which is obvious but it makes you think of her getting the blood on her hands which is disgusting especially when the writer says that 'it was damp'. She works it out quite slowly so it helps to make this part of the story really dramatic and tense.

| comments on the effect of the writer's choices |

| supports key idea with a quotation from the text |

| comments on the impact of the writer's choices on the reader |

(2) How much of this paragraph is **not** effective? Draw a line ✎ through any parts of the paragraph which:

- are repetitive – they say something that has already been said
- do not help to answer the question.

Your turn!

You are now going to write ✏ your own answer in response to the exam-style question.

> ### Exam-style question
>
> In lines 12–21, how does the writer use language and structure to show what has happened in the upstairs room?
>
> Support your views with reference to the text. **(6 marks)**

1 You will have 10–15 minutes in the exam to answer this kind of question so you should aim to write **three** paragraphs. Use these tasks to plan your response:

a Look carefully at the lines you are being asked to analyse in the source on page 10.

b Choose the **three** sentences from those lines that you find the most interesting and effective and copy ✏ them in the first row of the table below.

c Circle Ⓐ the words, phrases or parts of each sentence that you find the most interesting and effective.

d How could you comment on the writer's choices of language in the text you have circled? Note ✏ some ideas under your chosen sentences in the table below.

Sentences			
Comments			

2 Use your notes above to write ✏ your response to the exam-style question above on paper.

Review your skills

Check up

Review your response to the exam-style question on page 15. Tick ✓ the column to show how well you think you have done each of the following.

	Not quite ✓	Nearly there ✓	Got it! ✓
identified relevant ideas	☐	☐	☐
selected short, relevant quotations	☐	☐	☐
analysed the effect and impact on the reader of the writer's choices	☐	☐	☐

Need more practice?

Here is another exam-style question, this time relating to text 1 on page 73: an extract from *The Cold Hand* by Felix Octavius Carr Darley. You'll find some suggested points to refer to in the Answers section.

Exam-style question

In lines 22–35, how does the writer use language and structure to show the narrator is afraid?

Support your views with reference to the text.   (6 marks)

How confident do you feel about each of these **skills?** Colour ✏ in the bars.

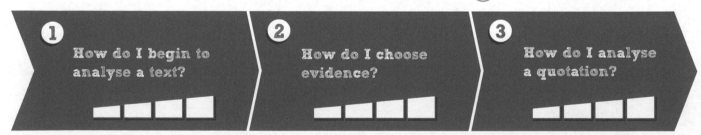

1 How do I begin to analyse a text?

2 How do I choose evidence?

3 How do I analyse a quotation?

Get started

Explain, comment on and analyse how writers use language and structure to achieve effects and influence readers (AO2)

③ Commenting on language

This unit will help you comment on language. The skills you will build are to:

- identify significant vocabulary choices in a text
- explore their effect and their impact on the reader
- structure your comments on the writer's vocabulary choices.

In the exam, you will face questions like the one below. This is about the text on page 18. This unit will prepare you to write your own response to this question, focusing on the writer's use of language. Unit 4 focuses on how to analyse the writer's use of structure.

Exam-style question

Analyse how the writer uses language and structure to interest and engage readers.

Support your views with detailed reference to the text. **(15 marks)**

The three key questions in the **skills boosts** will help you comment on language.

① How do I start to think about commenting on language?

② How do I choose which language to write about?

③ How do I comment on the writer's use of language?

Read the extract on page 18 from *The Life of Ian Fleming* by John Pearson, published in 1966. You will tackle a 20th-century non-fiction extract in the Reading section of your Paper 2 exam.

As you read, remember the following: ✓

 Check you understand the focus of the exam question you are preparing to respond to.

 Think about how the writer tries to interest and engage the reader.

 Mark or underline any language choices in the text which **you** find interesting or engaging.

Just before his first marriage at the age of 43, Ian Fleming wrote the first James Bond novel, *Casino Royale*.

Text 1 The Life of Ian Fleming, John Pearson

James Bond was born at **Goldeneye** on the morning of the third Tuesday of January 1952, when Ian Fleming had just finished breakfast and had ten more weeks of his forty-three years as a bachelor still to run. He had already had his swim out to the reef, and he was wearing white shorts, a coloured beach shirt from Antonio's in Falmouth, and black hide sandals. He came up the steps from the garden while **Violet** was clearing away the remains of
5   breakfast, shut the door of the big living room, closed the **jalousies**, and settled himself down at the brown roll-top desk with his oxidized gold cigarette case, his twenty-year-old **Imperial portable**, and a ream of best quality folio typing paper he had bought at a shop on Madison Avenue ten days earlier.

He had already **appropriated** the name of his hero: James Bond's handbook, *Birds of the West Indies*, was one of the books he liked to keep on his breakfast-table. 'I wanted the simplest, dullest, plainest-sounding name I could
10   find,' he said later. 'James Bond seemed perfect.'

Apart from the name he had no notes and had made no preparations for his story. He simply began to type in his cool, big, shaded room, and for the next seven weeks he kept at it steadily. Every morning between nine and twelve, while **Anne** was in the garden in a large straw hat painting flowers, the sound of the machine echoed through the still house. There were no distractions.

15   Around midday the noise of typing would cease and Fleming would come out of the house and sit yawning and blinking in the strong sunlight by the cliff. He liked to sun himself, usually with his shirt off, before lunch. After he had eaten he slept for an hour or so. At five he returned to his desk to read through what he had written before putting the pages into the blue manilla folder in the bottom left-hand drawer of the desk. By six thirty he was ready for his first real drink of the day.

20   On March 18th, six days before the marriage at Port Maria, the manilla folder was full. Le Chiffre was destroyed and Vesper Lynd was dead as well. Bond had scored his first recorded triumph, and the 62,000 words of one of the strangest thrillers ever written were finished. Probably never before has a book that has sold so well been produced quite so effortlessly…

There were corrections and additions still to be made to the typescript – more with *Casino Royale* than with any of
25   the subsequent books he wrote – and the changes are observable in the first manuscript, which Fleming lovingly preserved and had bound in blue **morocco** and embossed with his initials in gold. There is not a page without its maze of corrections in his strong, forward-sloping handwriting. Many paragraphs have been re-written and pages retyped and pasted in.

Yet it is clear that the whole story was there from the beginning – Bond and his world, the heroine, the casino,
30   the torture scene, the death of the two Bulgars – all came complete as he rattled the story down with such swift assurance at about 2,000 words a day.

Goldeneye: Ian Fleming's house in Jamaica
Violet: Ian Fleming's housekeeper
jalousies: shutters
Imperial portable: a typewriter
appropriated: borrowed
Anne: Fleming's fiancée, later his wife
morocco: a fine leather

How do I start to think about commenting on language?

Before you can comment on the impact of the writer's use of language, you need to think about the impact that the text has on **you**.

① Re-read the extract on page 18 and think about what the writer is writing about and the impressions the writer gives you of his subject.

a Which of the following does the writer write about in the extract? Cross ⊗ any that are **not** featured in the extract.

A.
☐ Ian Fleming: his personality and lifestyle

B.
☐ How Ian Fleming wrote his novel

C.
☐ The novel, *Casino Royale*

D.
☐ James Bond

E.
☐ Fleming's fiancée, Anne

F.
☐ Fleming's house in Jamaica, Goldeneye

G.
☐ Fleming's housekeeper, Violet

H.
☐ Fleming's childhood

b Look again at the things the writer writes about in the extract in part a. Which ones does the writer give the most attention, for example, the ones that you get the most information about and the clearest impression of from the text? Choose **three** and tick ✓ them, then write ✐ them in the 'focuses' column of the table below.

c Look at your three focuses. Think about the impressions that the text gives you of each one. Note down ✐ **three** words or phrases to sum up the impressions you get of each one from the text.

The three main focuses of the text are:	The impressions I get of them are:		

2 How do I choose which language to write about?

When you have identified the impressions the writer has given you in the text, you need to look more closely at the text to identify the paragraph, then the sentence and then the word or phrase that most strongly created that impression.

(1) Look at one student's notes on the impression she got of Ian Fleming from the extract on page 18.

> *Ian Fleming*
> * *Likes expensive things – he lives a life of luxury*
> * *Has a strict routine – he does the same thing every day*

☐
☐

a Which of the student's impressions above do you get most strongly from the section of the text below? Tick ✓ it.

> He had already had his swim out to the reef, and he was wearing white shorts, a coloured beach shirt from Antonio's in Falmouth, and black hide sandals. He came up the steps from the garden while Violet was clearing away the remains of breakfast, shut the door of the big living room, closed the jalousies, and settled himself down at the brown roll-top desk with his oxidized gold cigarette case, his twenty-year-old Imperial portable, and a ream of best quality folio typing paper he had bought at a shop on Madison Avenue ten days earlier.

b Think about the impression of Ian Fleming that you ticked above. Which **sentence** in the section of text gives you that impression most strongly? Underline Ⓐ it.

c Which **word or phrase** in the sentence that you have underlined creates that impression most strongly? Circle Ⓐ it.

d Write 🖉 **one or two** sentences explaining why the word or phrase that you have circled creates that impression.

....
....
....
....
....
....
....

(2) Now look closely at lines 29 to 31 in the extract on page 18.

Which **two** words or phrases most strongly give you the impression that Ian Fleming wrote his novel quickly?

....
....

How do I comment on the writer's use of language?

When you have identified a word or phrase that the writer has used to create a strong impression, you need to comment on **how** that vocabulary choice creates that impression. Think about:

- what that word or phrase **suggests** or **implies**
- what that word or phrase makes you **think** or **feel**.

① Look at the beginning of the extract on page 18.

> James Bond was born at Goldeneye on the morning of the third Tuesday of January 1952

James Bond is a fictional character, created by Ian Fleming. Why do you think the writer of the text chose to use the word `born` ? What does the word or phrase suggest?

a Look at some students' suggestions. Which ones do you agree with? Tick ✓ them.

Student A ☐
> It suggests that James Bond is a baby.

Student B ☐
> It suggests that Bond was actually born, not just imagined.

Student C ☐
> It suggests that Ian Fleming is like a parent who gave birth to James Bond.

b Now think about the impact that the word `born` might have on the reader. Look at some students' suggestions. Which ones do you agree with? Tick ✓ them.

Student A ☐
> It makes me think this was an important event.

Student B ☐
> It makes me feel that Ian Fleming was a really good writer.

Student C ☐
> It makes me feel that James Bond was almost like a real person.

Student D ☐
> It makes me think that writing a story is like giving birth to a living thing.

② Now look at the final sentence of the extract on page 18.

> Yet it is clear that the whole story was there from the beginning – Bond and his world, the heroine, the casino, the torture scene, the death of the two Bulgars – all came complete as he rattled the story down with such swift assurance at about 2,000 words a day.

Why do you think the writer chose the word `rattled` instead of, for example, 'wrote'? Think about:

- what the word suggests or implies about the way Ian Fleming wrote his story
- what the word makes you think or feel about Ian Fleming and his writing.

Write ✐ **one or two** sentences analysing the writer's use of words, phrases and language features in the final sentence above.

....

....

....

Commenting on language

To comment on language successfully, you need to:

- identify the writer's **focus**: what are the key points or ideas in the text?
- think about the **impressions** you get from the text, focusing on those key points or ideas
- identify the sections of the text, then the sentences, then the **words or phrases** in those sentences that most strongly give you those impressions
- comment on those words or phrases, thinking about **what they suggest** and **what they make you think or feel**.

Now look at this exam-style question, which you saw at the start of the unit.

Exam-style question

Analyse how the writer uses language and structure to interest and engage readers.

Support your views with detailed reference to the text.

(15 marks)

Look at this paragraph from one student's response to the question.

identifies a key idea in the text

explains the impression created

comments on what the word or phrase suggests

One way the writer interests the reader is by showing what Ian Fleming was like. The writer creates the impression that Fleming had a strict routine when he wrote his stories. The writer explains that Fleming would write his story 'Every morning between nine and twelve'. The phrase 'every morning' suggests he did the same thing every day which makes me think he was a very organised and determined person.

identifies a word or phrase that creates that impression

uses key words from the question

comments on what the word or phrase makes the reader think or feel

(1) Can you identify the different features of this student's response? Underline (A) the relevant parts of the paragraph, then link (✎) the annotations to them.

Your turn!

You are now going to write your own answer in response to the exam-style question, focusing on the writer's use of language. (Unit 4 focuses on how to analyse the writer's use of structure.)

Exam-style question

Analyse how the writer uses language and structure to interest and engage readers.

Support your views with detailed reference to the text. **(15 marks)**

(1) You should aim to write at least **three** paragraphs in response to this question. Use these tasks to complete a planning table like the one below.

a Write (✐) **three** things the writer **focuses** on in **lines 1–19** of the text.

b What **impression** does the writer create of each one? (✐)

c Identify (✐) the **word or phrase that most strongly** creates that impression of each one.

d Note down (✐) your ideas about what each word or phrase **suggests or implies**.

e Note down (✐) your ideas about what each word or phrase **makes you think or feel**.

Writer's focus	Impression created	Strong word or phrase	Suggestion or implication	Effect on reader

(2) Use your notes to write (✐) your response to the exam-style question above on paper.

Review your skills

Review your response to the exam style question on page 23. Tick ✓ the column to show how well you think you have done each of the following.

	Not quite ✓	Nearly there ✓	Got it! ✓
written about the key ideas in the text and the impressions created of them	☐	☐	☐
identified words and phrases that help to create those impressions	☐	☐	☐
commented on what those words or phrases suggest or imply	☐	☐	☐
commented on what those words or phrases make me think or feel	☐	☐	☐

Need more practice?

Here is another exam-style question, this time relating to text 3 on page 75: an extract from *Going Commando* by Mark Time. You'll find some suggested points to refer to in the Answers section.

Exam-style question

Analyse how the writer uses language and structure to interest and engage readers.

Support your views with detailed reference to the text.

(15 marks)

How confident do you feel about each of these **skills?** Colour 🖉 in the bars.

1 How do I start to think about commenting on language?

2 How do I choose which language to write about?

3 How do I comment on the writer's use of language?

④ Commenting on structure

This unit will help you comment on structure. The skills you will build are to:

* identify and explore how the writer has structured a text
* identify and explore significant choices of sentence structure in a text
* build effective comments on the writer's use of structure in a text.

In the exam, you will face questions like the one below. This is about the text on page 26. This unit will prepare you to write your own response to this question, focusing on the writer's use of structure. (Unit 3 focuses on how to analyse the writer's use of language.)

Exam-style question

Analyse how the writer uses language and structure to interest and engage readers.

Support your views with detailed reference to the text.

(15 marks)

The three key questions in the **skills boosts** will help you comment on structure.

1 How do I identify the effects of whole text structure?

2 How do I identify the effects of sentence structure choices?

3 How do I comment on the writer's use of structure?

Read the extract on page 26 from *Death in the Dust*, an article by John Steinbeck, published in 1936. You will tackle a 20th-century non-fiction extract in the Reading section of your Paper 2 exam.

As you read, remember the following: ⊘

Check you understand the focus of the exam question you are preparing to respond to.	Think about how the writer has selected ideas and information to interest and engage the reader.	Think about how the writer has structured the text and his sentences to add impact to the ideas and information.

In the Great Depression of the 1930s, thousands of Americans moved to California looking for work. They travelled around the country, staying wherever they found work and living in camps.

Text 1 Death in the Dust, John Steinbeck

The **squatters'** camps are located all over California. Let us see what a typical one is like. It is located on the banks of a river, near an irrigation ditch or on a side road where a spring of water is available. From a distance it looks like a city dump, and well it may, for the city dumps are the sources for the material of which it is built. You can see a litter of dirty rags and scrap iron, of houses built of weeds, of flattened cans or of paper. It is only on close
5 approach that it can be seen that these are homes.

Here is a house built by a family who have tried to maintain a neatness. The house is about 10 feet by 10 feet, and it is built completely of corrugated paper. The roof is peaked, the walls are tacked to a wooden frame. The dirt floor is swept clean, and along the irrigation ditch or in the muddy river the wife of the family scrubs clothes without soap and tries to rinse out the mud in muddy water.

10 The spirit of this family is not quite broken, for the children, three of them, still have clothes, and the family possesses three old quilts and a soggy, lumpy mattress. But the money so needed for food cannot be used for soap nor for clothes.

With the first rain the carefully built house will slop down into a brown, pulpy mush; in a few months the clothes will fray off the children's bodies, while the lack of nourishing food will subject the whole family to pneumonia
15 when the first cold comes. Five years ago this family had 50 acres of land and $1,000 in the bank. The wife belonged to a **sewing circle** and the man was a member of the **Grange**. They raised chickens, pigs, pigeons and vegetables and fruit for their own use; and their land produced the tall corn of the middle west. Now they have nothing.

If the husband hits every harvest without delay and works the maximum time, he may make $400 this year. But
20 if anything happens, if his old car breaks down, if he is late and misses a harvest or two, he will have to feed his whole family on as little as $150. But there is still pride in this family. Wherever they stop they try to put the children in school. It may be that the children will be in a school for as much as a month before they are moved to another locality.

There is more filth here. The tent is full of flies clinging to the apple box that is the dinner table, buzzing about
25 the foul clothes of the children, particularly the baby, who has not been bathed nor cleaned for several days. This family has been on the road longer than the builder of the paper house. There is no toilet here, but there is a clump of willows nearby where human faeces lie exposed to the flies – the same flies that are in the tent.

Two weeks ago there was another child, a four-year-old boy. For a few weeks they had noticed that he was kind of lackadaisical, that his eyes had been feverish. They had given him the best place in the bed, between father and
30 mother. But one night he went into convulsions and died, and the next morning the coroner's wagon took him away. It was one step down.

squatters: people who live in a house or on unoccupied land without permission
sewing circle: a group of people who meet regularly to sew, often making clothing to donate to charities
the Grange: a large group of farmers who worked together to buy and share farm machinery

How do I identify the effects of whole text structure?

Look at all the different ideas and information that the writer has chosen to include in a text. **How those ideas are linked** and **how they develop and change** in the text can have a significant impact on your impressions of a text and how it makes you think or feel.

(1) Look at one student's list of the key ideas and information in the extract on page 26.

Death in the Dust

> Details about a squatters' camp.

> Details about one family's house in the camp.

> Details about the family who live in the house.

> Details about the family's life when they had plenty of money and were successful.

> Details about another family that live in a tent in the camp.

> Details about their four-year-old son's death.

Now think about your first impressions of the text. How do you think the writer wants you to think and feel about the things he is describing in the text? Write ✐ **one** sentence summing up your ideas.

....

....

(a) Which of the patterns below can you spot in the structure of the text? Tick ✓ them.

☐	time	describing people or a place over a period of time
☐	travel	moving around a place observing all the different sights, sounds and smells
☐	contrast	two very different ideas or descriptions emphasise a great change or the difference between them
☐	narrowing focus	moving from a general impression of a person or place and then focusing more closely on details, like a camera zooming in

(b) Choose **one** of the patterns you have identified. How does it help to create or add to the first impressions you noted earlier in question (1)? Write ✐ **one or two** sentences explaining your ideas.

....

....

....

....

② How do I identify the effects of sentence structure choices?

How writers structure their sentences can have a significant impact on your impressions of a text and how it makes you think or feel.

① One of the key features of sentence structure is **sentence length**. Look at some of the longer and shorter sentences from the extract on page 26.

> They raised chickens, pigs, pigeons and vegetables and fruit for their own use; and their land produced the tall corn of the middle west. Now they have nothing.

> But one night he went into convulsions and died, and the next morning the coroner's wagon took him away. It was one step down.

Now look at some students' comments on the effects created by the structure of these sentences.

Student A This short sentence adds emphasis to the point that the writer is making.

Student B This short sentence makes this point even more dramatic.

Student C This longer sentence helps to make the writer's point by giving a long list of details.

Student D This longer sentence lists a series of events, suggesting how quickly and dramatically they happened.

Student E The contrasting length of these two sentences emphasises the contrast in the two things he is writing about.

a Use the students' comments to label ✏ the sentences in the extracts above with 'A', 'B', 'C', 'D' or 'E' to show what effect each sentence has.

b Now look at these two sentences from the extract on page 26.

> There is more filth here. The tent is full of flies clinging to the apple box that is the dinner table, buzzing about the foul clothes of the children, particularly the baby, who has not been bathed nor cleaned for several days.

How does the structure of **one** or **both** of these sentences add to your impressions of the place being described and your thoughts and feelings about it? Write ✏ **one or two** sentences explaining your ideas.

....

....

....

....

How do I comment on the writer's use of structure?

When you have identified a significant feature of the whole text's structure or a significant sentence structure, you need to comment on its effect. Think about:

- the impact of the writer's choice of structure
- how it adds to your impressions, thoughts and feelings about the text.

① Look at these sentences from the extract on page 26.

> The wife belonged to a sewing circle and the man was a member of the Grange. They raised chickens, pigs, pigeons and vegetables and fruit for their own use; and their land produced the tall corn of the middle west.

a Look at some students' comments on the impact of this part of the text. Which comments do you think are effective? Tick ✓ them.

Student A ☐

This section of the text is a really strong contrast with the rest of the text, pointing out what they used to have and what they have now.

Student B ☐

The writer uses a longer sentence to show all the things they had before they lost them all.

Student C ☐

The writer uses a list to emphasise how much they had and how much they have lost.

b Now look at some students' comments on how this part of the text adds to their impressions, thoughts or feelings about the text. Which ones do you agree with? Tick ✓ them.

Student A ☐

It makes you realise how living in the camp would be just as shocking for them as it is for the reader.

Student B ☐

The writer uses these details to make you feel even more sympathy for these people.

Student C ☐

It makes you realise how successful they were before they had to live in the camp.

② Now look at the **next** sentence from the extract.

> The wife belonged to a sewing circle and the man was a member of the Grange. They raised chickens, pigs, pigeons and vegetables and fruit for their own use; and their land produced the tall corn of the middle west. Now they have nothing.

Write ✏ **one or two** sentences analysing the writer's use of structure in this sentence. Think about:

- the impact of this short sentence structure
- how it adds to your impressions, thoughts or feelings about the text.

....

....

....

Commenting on structure

To comment effectively on the writer's use of structure, you need to:

- identify all the different ideas and information in the text and think about how they are linked or how they develop and change
- identify any significant sentence structures in the text: for example, longer sentences listing details or a sequence of events; shorter sentences used to add drama or emphasis to key ideas
- think about how the writer's choices of whole text structure or sentence structure create or add to your impressions of the text
- write about the impact of the writer's choice of structure and how it adds to your impressions, thoughts and feelings about the text.

Now look at the exam-style question which you saw at the start of the unit.

Exam-style question

Analyse how the writer uses language and structure to interest and engage readers.

Support your views with detailed reference to the text.

(15 marks)

Look at this paragraph from one student's response to the question.

uses key words from the question

explains the impression created

uses evidence to support the impression created

> The writer engages and interests the reader by making the reader feel sorry for the people living in the camp. At the start of the text he describes the camp. He says 'From a distance it looks like a city dump'. Then he focuses in on one house and the people who have to live there in a house made of corrugated paper. This means you feel like you are with the writer walking up to the camp and then looking at the houses and then the people. It makes you sympathise with the people in the camp because you see the way they have to live.

comments on the impact of the writer's choice of structure

comments on what the writer's choice of structure makes the reader think or feel

① Can you identify the different features of this student's response? Underline Ⓐ the relevant parts of the paragraph then link 🖊 the annotations to them.

Your turn!

You are now going to write your own answer in response to the exam-style question, focusing on the writer's use of structure. (Unit 3 focuses on how to analyse the writer's use of language.)

Exam-style question

Analyse how the writer uses language and structure to interest and engage readers.

Support your views with detailed reference to the text. **(15 marks)**

(1) You should aim to write at least **two** paragraphs in response to this question about the extract on page 26. Use these tasks to complete the planning table below.

   a Note down ✏ **one** significant feature of the **whole text structure** of the extract.

   b Note down ✏ **one** significant **sentence structure** from the extract.

   c Note down ✏ your ideas about the impact of each structural feature.

   d Note down ✏ your ideas about how that structural feature adds to your impressions, thoughts or feelings about the text.

A significant feature of whole text structure	The impact of that feature	How it adds to my impressions, thoughts or feelings

A significant feature of sentence structure	The impact of that feature	How it adds to my impressions, thoughts or feelings

(2) Use your notes to write ✏ your response to the exam-style question above on paper.

Unit 4 Commenting on structure   **31**

Review your skills

Check up

Review your response to the exam-style question on page 31. Tick ✓ the column to show how well you think you have done each of the following.

	Not quite ✓	Nearly there ✓	Got it! ✓
identified a significant feature of whole text structure	☐	☐	☐
identified a significant sentence structure	☐	☐	☐
commented on the impact of each structural feature	☐	☐	☐
commented on how each structural feature adds to my impressions, thoughts or feelings about the text	☐	☐	☐

Look over all of your work in this chapter. Note down ✏ the **three** most important things to remember when commenting on structure.

1. ....

2. ....

3. ....

Need more practice?

Below is another exam-style question, this time relating to text 2 on page 74: an extract from *The Battle of the Somme*. You'll find some suggested points to refer to in the Answers section.

Exam-style question

Analyse how the writer uses language and structure to interest and engage readers.

Support your views with detailed reference to the text.

(15 marks)

How confident do you feel about each of these **skills?** Colour ✏ in the bars.

1 How do I identify the effects of whole text structure?

2 How do I identify the effects of sentence structure choices?

3 How do I comment on the writer's use of structure?

Explain, comment on and analyse how writers use language and structure to achieve effects and influence readers (AO2)

⑤ Commenting on language and structure

This unit will help you comment on both language and structure together. The skills you will build are to:

- understand how to tackle questions that ask you to comment on language and structure
- select evidence that will allow you to comment on both language and structure
- build effective comments on the writer's use of language and structure.

In the exam, you will face questions like the one below. This is about the text on page 34. This unit will prepare you to write your own response to this question.

The three key questions in the **skills boosts** will help you comment on language and structure.

 How do I write about language and structure?

 How do I choose the best evidence for commenting on language and structure?

 How do I comment on language and structure?

Read the text on page 34: *I Fell Out of the Sky*, an article published in the *Guardian* in 2014. You will tackle a 21st-century non-fiction extract in the Reading section of your Paper 2 exam.

As you read, remember the following: ✓

Check you understand the focus of the exam question you are preparing to respond to.	Think about how the writer has selected ideas and information, and used sentence structures and vocabulary choices to interest and engage the reader.	Mark or underline any ideas or information, sentence structures or vocabulary choices that **you** find interesting or engaging.

In this newspaper article, Neil Laughton describes a terrifying experience.

Text 1 | Fell Out of the Sky, The Guardian

It is not true that your life flashes before your eyes when you're seconds from death. As I hurtled to mine at 60mph, I felt nothing but panic, fear and a deep pang of regret. The earth rushing towards me, I braced for impact. Then the world went black.

5 Moments earlier I had been on top of the world – soaring and swooping at 50mph like a bird, skimming over lakes, hopping over trees. I was paramotoring – a bit like paragliding, but with a caged engine and propeller strapped to my back. It is a beautiful feeling to be suspended in a floating chair, steering with two cords. At one with the elements, you are defying Newton's laws. It's the ultimate freedom, the ultimate rush.

Paramotoring was a relatively new sport in 2006. My team and I were in Chamonix, in the French Alps, practising for a bid to become the first to fly a paramotor to a record-breaking altitude of over 13,000ft in the Himalayas the 10 following year.

It was Easter Saturday and the plan was to practise stalling and spinning, which involved collapsing and reinflating the canopy at a minimum of 1,000ft. It would prepare us for any emergency on record-attempt day.

After lunch, I volunteered to take off again first from the launch site. The skies were blue and I could see the Alps stretching over the horizon. I had reached only about 100ft and, with a farmhouse in my line of sight, I knew I 15 needed to climb higher to pass it safely. I pulled the brake lines to increase the angle of the wing for extra lift. But I forgot I had tightened them before takeoff and made them far more sensitive. I pulled too hard. That, combined with the **eddies** swirling from the trees and buildings ahead, caused a break in the airflow under the canopy. Instantly, it began to deflate.

I had just enough time to look up and see the thin material of my wing falling towards me like an enormous bunch 20 of useless laundry. I was dropping like a stone.

Tumbling through the air with no way to stop is a sensation of utter helplessness: a truly stomach-churning moment where you know you're not going forwards or upwards; you're just falling. There's no time to think. One second became two, two became three. I closed my eyes. Wallop.

When I came to, I was on my back with cabbage in my mouth. I was lying in a vegetable patch, surrounded by 25 squashed lettuces, broccoli and cabbages. I felt dazed. About 15ft away, I noticed a French family sitting on their patio eating breakfast. Their coffees and croissants halfway to their open mouths, they just sat there staring.

By my left shoulder was a Calor gas canister that, if I had landed on it, could have blown me up. And six inches to my right was an eight-foot steel spike, sharpened at the end. By some incredible twist of good fortune, I'd landed between the two. I couldn't understand how I was still alive. Then I noticed the roof of the farmhouse. It was 30 obliterated, still showering the ground with shattered tiles.

It was the roof that saved my life. The house was 50ft tall and broke my fall. If you throw a tortoise in the air, it will revolve and land on its heaviest element – its shell. The paramotor was my shell, breaking my fall when I hit the roof and then the cabbage patch.

I didn't go to hospital, because incredibly I had no broken bones. I was bruised and shaken but otherwise fine. So I 35 got up, brushed myself down and walked over to apologise to the family, who were rather decent about it, asking only for €500 to repair the roof.

eddies: swirling winds that make aircraft very difficult to control

1 How do I write about language and structure?

When you analyse the writer's use of language and structure, not every paragraph you write has to comment on both. Some of your paragraphs could focus on language, others on structure. However, you do need to comment on both at some point in your response.

① Look at these three short extracts from one student's comments on the writer's use of language and structure in the text on page 34.

A.

The writer begins the article describing how he thought he was going to die: 'As I hurtled to mine at 60mph, I felt nothing but panic, fear and a deep pang of regret'. Putting this at the start of the article grabs the reader's attention because the word 'hurtled' shows how fast he was going and it sounds like he was out of control.

B.

As he crashes, he writes: 'Then the world went black.' This short sentence makes him hitting the ground sound really sudden and dramatic.

C.

The writer shows how quickly things changed: 'Moments earlier I had been on top of the world – soaring and swooping at 50mph like a bird, skimming over lakes, hopping over trees'. The words 'soaring' and 'swooping' make him sound free and joyful.

a Which of the comments above focus on language only? Label 🖉 them 'L' in the first column of boxes.

b Which of the comments above focus on structure only? Label 🖉 them 'S' in the first column of boxes.

c Which of the comments above focus on language **and** structure? Label 🖉 them 'S/L' in the first column of boxes.

d Which of the comments above is the most effective? Put a tick ✓ in the second column of boxes.

e Write 🖉 **one or two** sentences explaining why you chose that comment.

....

....

....

② a Look closely at the comments you labelled 'L'. What could you add to this comment about the writer's use of sentence structure in the quotation? Note 🖉 your ideas below.

....

....

b Look closely at the comments you labelled 'S'. What could you add to this comment about the writer's use of language in the quotation? Note 🖉 your ideas below.

....

....

② How do I choose the best evidence for commenting on language and structure?

To find the best evidence, you need to focus on parts of the text which create a strong impression, thought or feeling. You can then look closely at those parts of the text for sentence structures and vocabulary choices that you can explore and comment on.

① If you were asked to comment on the writer's use of language and structure in the article on page 34, you could focus on some or all of these impressions, thoughts and feelings that the writer tries to create.

A. | adventure and excitement | B. | danger and tension | C. | humour |

Which of the quotations below contributes strongly to the impressions, thoughts and feelings above? In the first column of boxes, label ✏ the quotations 'A', 'B' or 'C' – or 'X' if the quotation does not contribute to any of them.

i. | It's the ultimate freedom, the ultimate rush. | ☐ ☐

ii. | My team and I were in Chamonix, in the French Alps, practising for a bid to become the first to fly a paramotor to a record-breaking altitude of over 13,000ft in the Himalayas the following year. | ☐ ☐

iii. | I had just enough time to look up and see the thin material of my wing falling towards me like an enormous bunch of useless laundry. I was dropping like a stone. | ☐ ☐

iv. | When I came to, I was on my back with cabbage in my mouth. I was lying in a vegetable patch, surrounded by squashed lettuces, broccoli and cabbages. I felt dazed. | ☐ ☐

② If you wanted to comment on the writer's use of **sentence structure** (and how it contributes to the impression the writer creates in the text), which quotation would you choose? Label ✏ it 'S' in the second column of boxes.

③ If you wanted to comment on the writer's **language choice** (and how it contributes to the impression the writer creates in the text), which quotation would you choose? Label ✏ it 'L' in the second column of boxes.

④ Look at the quotation you labelled 'S'.

　ⓐ Can you find a word or phrase that adds to the impression created in the quotation? Circle Ⓐ it.

　ⓑ Write ✏ **one or two** sentences explaining its effect.

　...

　...

　...

⑤ Look again at the quotation you labelled 'L'. Does the structure of the sentence add to the impression created in the quotation? How? Write ✏ **one or two** sentences explaining your ideas.

　...

　...

　...

③ How do I comment on language and structure?

An effective comment on language and structure:
- identifies the impression the writer is trying to create in the text
- selects a quotation in which that impression is strongly created
- comments on how the writer's language choices in the quotation help to create that impression
- comments on how the writer's use of sentence structure in the quotation helps to create that impression.

① Look at some sentences from one student's comments on the use of language and structure in the article on page 34.

A.
☐ The writer creates the impression that paramotoring is exciting. ☐

B.
☐ The article makes you realise how lucky the writer was to escape with his life, and not even have to go to hospital. ☐

C.
☐ He says, 'It's the ultimate freedom, the ultimate rush'. ☐

D.
☐ The writer's language in this sentence makes it sound quite dangerous. ☐

E.
☐ The short sentence structure adds emphasis to the idea that it's a really extreme and exciting sport. ☐

F.
☐ Repeating the word 'ultimate' makes it sound like he really means it and is excited about it. ☐

G.
☐ The word 'freedom' makes it sound exciting. ☐

(a) Which of these sentences identify an impression the writer is trying to create? Label ✎ them 'I' in the first column of boxes.

(b) Which of these sentences comment on language? Label ✎ them 'L' in the first column of boxes.

(c) Which of these sentences comment on structure? Label ✎ them 'S' in the first column of boxes.

(d) Which of these sentences would you include in a paragraph focusing on how the writer uses **language** and **structure** to create the impression that paramotoring is **exciting**? Put a tick ✓ in the first column of boxes.

(e) Now think about how you would structure your paragraph. In what order would you sequence the sentences you have ticked? Number ✎ them in the second column of boxes.

Commenting on language and structure

To write an effective comment on language and structure you need to:

- identify an impression the writer is trying to create in the text
- select a quotation in which that impression is strongly created
- comment on how the writer's language choices in the quotation help to create that impression
- comment on how the writer's use of sentence structure in the quotation helps to create that impression.

Now look at the exam-style question about Text 1 on page 34.

Exam-style question

Analyse how the writer uses language and structure to interest and engage readers.

Support your views with detailed reference to the text.

(15 marks)

Look at this paragraph from one student's response to the question.

identifies a significant impression created in the text

comments on how sentence structure adds to the impression created

> The writer engages the reader by building up the tension as he describes falling to the ground: 'There's no time to think. One second became two, two became three. I closed my eyes. Wallop'. Using short sentences makes it sound like it is happening very quickly and like he is panicking. The last one of these short sentences is just one word 'Wallop'. This word makes you realise how hard he hit the ground and the short sentence makes you realise how everything stopped when he hit it.

uses key words from the question

identifies a significant language choice

identifies a significant sentence structure

comments on how language choice adds to the impression created

① Can you identify the different features of this student's response? Underline Ⓐ the relevant parts of the paragraph then link 🖉 the annotations to them.

Your turn!

You are now going to write your own answer in response to the exam-style question about Text 1 on page 34.

Exam-style question

Analyse how the writer uses language and structure to interest and engage readers.

Support your views with detailed reference to the text. **(15 marks)**

1 You should aim to write at least **two** paragraphs in response to this question. Use these tasks to complete the planning table below.

a Note down ✏ **two** impressions that the writer is trying to create in the article.

b Select ✏ **two** quotations in which those impressions are strongly created. Aim to choose quotations in which the writer's use of language and sentence structure contributes significantly to the impression created.

c Note down ✏ your ideas about the impact of sentence structure in your quotations.

d Note down ✏ your ideas about the impact of the writer's language choices in your quotations.

	Paragraph 1	Paragraph 2
Impressions created		
Quotations		
Comment on sentence structure		
Comment on language choice		

2 Use your notes to write ✏ your response to the exam-style question above on paper.

Review your skills

Check up

Review your response to the exam-style question on page 39. Tick ✓ the column to show how well you think you have done each of the following.

	Not quite ✓	Nearly there ✓	Got it! ✓
identified two different impressions the writer creates in the article	☐	☐	☐
selected relevant quotations	☐	☐	☐
commented on the writer's use of sentence structure	☐	☐	☐
commented on the writer's language choices	☐	☐	☐

Look over all of your work in this unit. Note down 🖉 the **three** most important things to remember when commenting on language and structure.

1. ....

2. ....

3. ....

Need more practice?

Below is another exam-style question, this time relating to Text 1 on page 73: an extract from *The Cold Hand* by Felix Octavius Carr Darley. You'll find some suggested points to refer to in the Answers section.

Exam-style question

In lines 5–14, how does the writer use language and structure to show that something strange and frightening is happening?

Support your views with reference to the text.

(6 marks)

How confident do you feel about each of these **skills?** Colour 🖉 in the bars.

1 How do I write about language and structure?

2 How do I choose the best evidence for commenting on language and structure?

3 How do I comment on language and structure?

⑥ Evaluating a text

This unit will help you evaluate a text. The skills you will build are to:

- recognise the writer's intentions
- identify where in the text the writer has attempted to achieve that intention
- comment on how the writer has achieved that intention
- write an evaluation.

In the exam, you will face questions like the one below. This is about the text on page 42. This unit will prepare you to write your own response to this question.

Exam-style question

In this extract, there is an attempt to build a sense of danger.

Evaluate how succesfully this is achieved.

Support your views with detailed reference to the text.   **(15 marks)**

The three key questions in the **skills boosts** will help you evaluate texts.

 1 How do I identify where the writer has tried to achieve their intention?

 2 How do I comment on the writer's intention?

 3 How do I evaluate the writer's success?

Read the extract on page 42 from *Dracula* by Bram Stoker, published in 1897.
You will tackle a 19th-century fiction extract in the Reading section of your Paper 1 exam.

As you read, remember the following:

Check you understand the focus of the exam question you are preparing to respond to.

Mark or highlight any parts of the text relevant to the question you are going to answer: where the writer creates a sense of danger.

Jonathan Harker has just arrived at a castle in the middle of the night. In this extract, Harker gives his first impressions of his host: Count Dracula.

Text 1 Dracula, Bram Stoker

By this time I had finished my supper, and by my host's desire had drawn up a chair by the fire and begun to smoke a cigar which he offered me, at the same time excusing himself that he did not smoke. I had now an opportunity of observing him, and found him **of a very marked physiognomy.**

His face was a strong, a very strong, **aquiline**, with high bridge of the thin nose and peculiarly arched nostrils,
5   with lofty domed forehead, and hair growing scantily round the temples but profusely elsewhere. His eyebrows were very massive, almost meeting over the nose, and with bushy hair that seemed to curl in its own profusion. The mouth, so far as I could see it under the heavy moustache, was fixed and rather cruel-looking, with peculiarly sharp white teeth.

These protruded over the lips, whose remarkable ruddiness showed astonishing vitality in a man of his years. For
10   the rest, his ears were pale, and at the tops extremely pointed. The chin was broad and strong, and the cheeks firm though thin. The general effect was one of extraordinary **pallor**.

Hitherto I had noticed the backs of his hands as they lay on his knees in the firelight, and they had seemed rather white and fine. But seeing them now close to me, I could not but notice that they were rather coarse, broad, with squat fingers. Strange to say, there were hairs in the centre of the palm. The nails were long and fine, and cut to
15   a sharp point. As the Count leaned over me and his hands touched me, I could not repress a shudder. It may have been that his breath was rank, but a horrible feeling of nausea came over me, which, do what I would, I could not conceal.

The Count, evidently noticing it, drew back. And with a grim sort of smile, which showed more than he had yet done his protruberant teeth, sat himself down again on his own side of the fireplace. We were both silent for a
20   while, and as I looked towards the window I saw the first dim streak of the coming dawn. There seemed a strange stillness over everything. But as I listened, I heard as if from down below in the valley the howling of many wolves. The Count's eyes gleamed, and he said.

"Listen to them, the children of the night. What music they make!" Seeing, I suppose, some expression in my face strange to him, he added, "Ah, sir, you dwellers in the city cannot enter into the feelings of the hunter." Then he
25   rose and said:

"But you must be tired. Your bedroom is all ready, and tomorrow you shall sleep as late as you will. I have to be away till the afternoon, so sleep well and dream well!" With a courteous bow, he opened for me himself the door to the octagonal room, and I entered my bedroom.

of a very marked physiognomy: to have very unusual facial features
aquiline: like an eagle
pallor: paleness
hitherto: until now

1 How do I identify where the writer has tried to achieve their intention?

In every text, the writer has an intention: the impact they want their text to have on the reader. To evaluate a text, you need to focus on the **writer's intention** and identify **where in the text the writer has achieved it.**

① The question you are going to answer gives you one student's ideas about the writer's intention.

Exam-style question

In this extract, there is an attempt to build a sense of danger.

Evaluate how succesfully this is achieved.

To respond to this question, you need to work out where in the text **the writer builds a sense of danger**. In this extract, the writer includes.

A. the narrator's description of Count Dracula

B. the narrator's thoughts and feelings

C. a conversation between the narrator and Count Dracula.

Which of these helps to create a sense of danger? Tick ✓ them.

② Look at some of the things we are told about Count Dracula. Which ones suggest that Count Dracula could be a dangerous character? Tick ✓ them.

A. His eyebrows were massive, almost meeting over the nose.

B. there were hairs in the centre of the palm. The nails were long and fine, and cut to a sharp point.

C. The mouth, so far as I could see it under the heavy moustache, was fixed and rather cruel-looking, with peculiarly sharp white teeth.

③ Now look at the some of the things the narrator tells us about his thoughts and feelings. Which ones suggest that he feels a sense of danger? Tick ✓ them.

A. I could not repress a shudder. It may have been that his breath was rank, but a horrible feeling of nausea came over me

B. as I looked towards the window I saw the first dim streak of the coming dawn. There seemed a strange stillness over everything.

C. Seeing, I suppose, some expression in my face strange to him,

④ Write ✎ **one or two** sentences summing up how the writer tries to build a sense of danger.

....

....

....

2 How do I comment on the writer's intention?

The best comments on the writer's intention do not simply say what the writer has done in the text: they comment on how the writer's choices help them to achieve their intention.

① The question you are going to answer focuses on the writer's intention to create a sense of danger.

Look at these sentences from the text on page 42:

> As the Count leaned over me and his hands touched me, I could not repress a shudder. It may have been that his breath was rank, but a horrible feeling of nausea came over me, which, do what I would, I could not conceal.

Which words and phrases in these sentences strongly suggest a sense of danger? Circle them. Ⓐ

② Now look at the one student's comments on this part of the text, written in response to the exam-style question above.

The writer describes how Dracula 'leaned over' and 'his hands touched me'.

It shows how close Dracula was to him and it feels uncomfortable.

The narrator says he 'could not repress a shudder'.

This makes you think he is frightened of Count Dracula.

The narrator describes the 'horrible feeling of nausea' he experiences.

It shows how strongly he reacts to the touch and smell of Dracula.

ⓐ Which comments explain what the writer has done in the text? Label 🖉 them **W**.

ⓑ Which comments explain how this helps the writer achieve his intention of building a sense of danger? Label 🖉 them **H**.

ⓒ Which ones do neither? Cross ⓧ them.

③ Now look at these sentences from the text on page 42.

> But as I listened, I heard as if from down below in the valley the howling of many wolves. The Count's eyes gleamed, and he said.
>
> "Listen to them, the children of the night. What music they make!"

ⓐ Which words and phrases strongly suggest a sense of danger? Circle Ⓐ them.

ⓑ Write 🖉 **one or two** sentences commenting on **what the writer has done** in the sentences above and **how it helps to build a sense of danger**.

....

....

....

....

....

③ How do I evaluate the writer's success?

To evaluate the success of a text, you need to comment on **how well** the writer has done what they set out to do: whether they have **achieved their intention**.

① Look at the beginning of a paragraph written by a student evaluating how successfully the writer builds a sense of danger.

> When wolves start howling at the end of the extract, Dracula's eyes gleam and he says: 'Listen to them, the children of the night. What music they make!'.

ⓐ You are going to build an effective comment to complete the paragraph.
Choose and tick ✓:

- **one** comment on what the writer has done
- **one** comment on how this helps the writer's intention
- **one** comment that evaluates how successfully it creates the writer's intended impact on the reader.

What has the writer done?	Dracula describes the wolves as 'children of the night'. ☐	Dracula describes the wolves' howling as 'music'. ☐	Dracula's speech ends with an exclamation. ☐
How does it help the writer's intention?	The word 'children' makes you think there is some connection between Dracula and the wolves. ☐	This suggests Dracula is not like most people who think wolves are dangerous and frightening. ☐	It suggests that Dracula is very excited by the wolves and their howling. ☐
Is it successful?	This clearly shows that Dracula is a strange and frightening character who could be dangerous. ☐	This really makes you feel that Dracula is as dangerous as the wolves. ☐	You strongly feel the tension and danger as Dracula talks and behaves in such a strange and disturbing way. ☐

ⓑ In what order would you sequence your three chosen sentences in your paragraph? Number 🖉 them.

ⓒ Read through and write 🖉 your chosen sentences on paper in your chosen order to make sure that they effectively comment on and evaluate the writer's choices.

Evaluating a text

To write a good evaluation, you need to:

- identify the writer's intention
- identify where in the text the writer has attempted to achieve their intention
- comment on what the writer has done and how it helps them to achieve their intention
- comment on the success of its impact on the reader.

Now look at the exam-style question about the text on page 42.

Exam-style question

In this extract, there is an attempt to build a sense of danger.

Evaluate how succesfully this is achieved.

Support your views with detailed reference to the text.

(15 marks)

Look at a paragraph written by one student in response to the exam-style question above.

| identifies where the writer has tried to achieve their intention | The narrator describes Count Dracula in a lot of detail. One of the most strange and frightening details is his nails: 'The nails were long and fine and cut to a sharp point'. Because they are 'cut to a sharp point', it makes you think he has nails that are a bit like claws and it makes you think of Dracula's sharp teeth and the wolves that are heard at the end of the extract. This really builds up the sense of danger because it feels like the narrator is sitting with a wild animal who could attack him at any minute. | comments on how what the writer has done helps the writer's intention |

comments on what the writer has done

comments on the success of its impact on the reader

① Can you identify all the different things the student has included in this paragraph? Link ✐ the annotations to the paragraph to show where the student has included them.

Your turn!

You are now going to write your own answer in response to the exam-style question.

Exam-style question

In this extract, there is an attempt to build a sense of danger.

Evaluate how succesfully this is achieved.

Support your views with detailed reference to the text.   (15 marks)

(1) You should aim to write at least **three** paragraphs in response to this question. Use these tasks to complete the planning table below.

   a Note down 🖊 **three points in the text** where the writer builds a sense of danger.

   b Choose 🖊 **one** quotation to support **each** of those points.

   c Note down 🖊 your ideas about what the writer has done in each quotation.

   d Note down 🖊 your ideas about how this helps the writer to achieve his intention.

   e Note down 🖊 your ideas about its impact on the reader and how successful this is.

	1	2	3
Points			
Quotations			
What has the writer done?			
How?			
Is it successful?			

Review your skills

Check up

Review your response to the exam-style question on page 47. Tick ✓ the column to show how well you think you have done each of the following.

	Not quite ✓	Nearly there ✓	Got it! ✓
identified where the writer has tried to achieve their intention	☐	☐	☐
commented on the writer's intention	☐	☐	☐
evaluated the writer's success	☐	☐	☐

Need more practice?

Here is another exam-style question, this time relating to Text 1 on page 73: an extract from *The Cold Hand* by Felix Octavius Carr Darley. You'll find some suggested points to refer to in the Answers section.

Exam-style question

In this extract, there is an attempt to show a frightening experience.

Evaluate how succesfully this is achieved.

Support your views with detailed reference to the text

(15 marks)

How confident do you feel about each of these **skills?** Colour 🖉 in the bars.

1 How do I identify where the writer has tried to achieve their intention?

2 How do I comment on the writer's intention?

3 How do I evaluate the writer's success?

(7) Synthesising and comparing

This unit will help you synthesise and compare information and ideas from two different texts. The skills you will build are to:

- identify relevant information in each text
- identify similarities in the key ideas and information in the two texts
- write a comparison of the key ideas and information in two texts.

In the exam, you will face questions like the one below. This is about the texts on page 50. This unit will prepare you to write your own response to this question.

Exam-style question

The two texts show the writers' experience of going to bed while staying at someone else's house.

What similarities do the writers' experiences share in these texts?

Use evidence from both texts to support your answer. **(6 marks)**

The three key questions in the **skills boosts** will help you synthesise and compare information and ideas in two texts.

 1 How do I identify points of comparison?

 2 How do I synthesise information and ideas in two texts?

 3 How do I write a comparison?

Read the extracts on page 50 from *Let Us Now Praise Famous Men* by James Agee and Walker Evans, published in 1941, and *The Life and Times of the Thunderbolt Kid* by Bill Bryson, published in 2006. You will tackle one 20th-century and one 21st-century non-fiction extract in the Reading section of your Paper 2 exam.

As you read, remember the following:

Check you understand the focus of the exam question you are preparing to respond to.

Mark or highlight any ideas and information in each text that is relevant to the exam question.

Consider any similarities or differences in the ideas and information in each text.

James Agee is living with a family of farmers struggling to survive in 1930s America..

Text 1 Let Us Now Praise Famous Men, James Agee and Walker Evans

I sat on the edge of the bed, turned out the lamp, and lay back along the outside of the covers. After a couple of minutes I got up, stripped, and slid in between the sheets. The bedding was saturated and full of chill as the air was. I could feel the thinness and lumpiness of the mattress and the weakness of the springs. The mattress was rustlingly noisy if I turned or contracted my body. I began to feel sharp little piercings and crawlings all along the

5 surface of my body. I itch a good deal at best: but it was bugs all right. I felt places growing on me and scratched at them, and they became unmistakable bedbug bites. I struck a match and a half dozen broke along my pillow: I caught two, killed them, and smelled their queer rankness. They were full of my blood. I struck another match and spread back the cover; they rambled off by dozens. I got out of bed, lighted the lamp, and scraped the palms of my hands all over my body, then went for the bed. I killed maybe a dozen in all; I couldn't find the rest; but I did

10 find fleas, and, along the seams of the pillow and mattress, small gray translucent brittle insects which I suppose were lice. I put on my coat, buttoned my pants outside it, put my socks on, got into bed, turned out the lamp, turned up my coat collar, wrapped my head in my shirt, stuck my hands under my coat at the chest, and tried to go to sleep.

Bill Bryson remembers staying at his grandparents' house as a child.

Text 2 The Life and Times of the Thunderbolt Kid, Bill Bryson

The sleeping porch was a slightly rickety, loosely enclosed porch on the back of the house that was only **notionally** separate from the outside world. It contained an ancient sagging bed that my grandfather slept in in the summer when the house was uncomfortably warm. But sometimes in the winter when the house was full of guests it was pressed into service, too.

5 The only heat in the sleeping porch was that of any human being who happened to be out there. It couldn't have been more than one or two degrees warmer than the world outside – and outside was perishing. So to sleep on the sleeping porch required preparation. First, you put on long underwear, pajamas, jeans, a sweatshirt, your grandfather's old cardigan and bathrobe, two pairs of woolen socks on your feet and another on your hands, and a hat with earflaps tied beneath the chin. Then you climbed into bed and were immediately covered with a dozen

10 bed blankets, three horse blankets, all the household overcoats, a canvas tarpaulin, and a piece of old carpet. I'm not sure that they didn't lay an old wardrobe on top of that, just to hold everything down. It was like sleeping under a dead horse. For the first minute or so it was unimaginably cold, shockingly cold, but gradually your body heat seeped in and you became warm and happy in a way you would not have believed possible only a minute or two before. It was bliss.

notionally: in theory, not in reality

How do I identify points of comparison?

To identify key points for comparison, you need to identify the key ideas and information in the two texts that are relevant to the task you are tackling.

1 Look at this exam-style question:

Exam-style question

The two texts show the writers' experience of going to bed while staying at someone else's house. What similarities do the writers' experiences share in these texts?

Now look at one student's notes identifying key ideas and information in the **first half** of each text:

Text 1: *Let Us Now Praise Famous Men*

A. | The writer lies down on top of the covers. He seems nervous of going to bed. |

B. | The bed is wet and cold. |

C. | The mattress is thin, lumpy and noisy. |

D. | The writer is bitten. The bed is infested with bed bugs. |

E. ....

F. ....

G. ....

Text 2: *The Life and Times of the Thunderbolt Kid*

A. | He is sleeping in a porch on the back of the house. |

B. | His grandfather slept in the bed on the porch when it was too hot in the house. |

C. | Sometimes the bed in the porch is used for guests. |

D. | The bed is ancient and sagging. |

E. | The porch is freezing cold. |

F. ....

G. ....

H. ....

a Which key ideas do **not** focus on | the writers' experiences of going to bed | and are therefore **not** relevant to the question? Cross ⊗ them.

b Look again at **Text 1** on page 50. Complete 🖉 the student's notes above, noting down all the key ideas and information in the **second half** of the text. Cross ⊗ any that are not relevant to the exam-style question.

c Look again at **Text 2** on page 50. Complete 🖉 the student's notes above, noting down all the key ideas and information in the **second half** of the text. Cross ⊗ any that are not relevant to the exam-style question.

2 How do I synthesise information and ideas in two texts?

When you synthesise information from texts in order to compare their differences:

- **don't** look for **identical** ideas
- **do** look for **similar** ideas.

(1) Look at one student's notes identifying the key ideas and information from Text 2, and giving a brief summary of those key ideas.

Text 2: The Life and Times of the Thunderbolt Kid
- He is sleeping in a porch on the back of the house.
- The bed is ancient and sagging.
- The porch is freezing cold.
- The writer puts on layers and layers of clothing to try to keep warm.
- The writer then has blankets, coats and a carpet put on him. It's like 'sleeping under a dead horse'.
- At first it is freezing but he soon warms up.

Text 2 Summary
The writer writes about:
- the mattress
- the temperature
- discomfort
- clothing and blankets
- warmth and comfort.

Now look at the student's notes on the key ideas and information in Text 1. Use them to write a brief summary of those key ideas.

Text 1: Let Us Now Praise Famous Men
- The writer lies down on top of the covers. He seems nervous of going to bed.
- The bed is wet and cold.
- The mattress is thin, lumpy and noisy.
- The writer is bitten. The bed is infested with bed bugs.
- He squashes the bed bugs. They smell and are full of blood.
- The writer also finds fleas and lice.
- The writer gets dressed and gets back into bed.

Text 1 Summary
The writer writes about:
- ....
- ....
- ....
- ....
- ....
- ....
- ....

(2) Compare the student's summary of Text 2 with your summary of Text 1. What **similarities** can you spot? Use your ideas to complete the sentences below, summing up **two** of the similarities in the texts.

a Both writers ....
....
....

b Both writers ....
....
....

3 How do I write a comparison?

A comparison should identify significant similarities and/or differences in the key ideas and information in the two texts, and support them using evidence from each text.

① Each comparison you make between two texts should be clearly stated at the start of the paragraph. For example:

> Both writers use clothing to make themselves more comfortable.

a Choose **one** relevant quotation from **each** text to support this point. Write 🖉 them below.

Text 1	Text 2

b Choose **two** key details from **each** of your quotations. Use them to complete 🖉 the sentences below:

In Text 1, the writer describes how he	In a similar way, the writer of Text 2 describes how he had to put on
and	

c You may need to explain the significance of your evidence from each source. Complete 🖉 the sentences below.

The writer of Text 1 does this to try to	This is because the writer of Text 2 is

Synthesising and comparing

To write a good comparison of the key ideas and information in two texts, you need to:
- identify all the relevant ideas and information in each text
- identify at least three points of comparison
- support each point in your comparison with short, relevant evidence from each text
- explain the significance of your chosen evidence in each text.

Now look at this exam-style question you saw at the start of the unit.

Exam-style question

The two texts show the writers' experience of going to bed while staying at someone else's house.

What similarities do the writers' experiences share in these texts?

Use evidence from both texts to support your answer. **(6 marks)**

Look at a paragraph written by one student in response to the exam-style question above.

identifies a key similarity in the two texts

supports the key point with evidence from Text 2

> In both texts, the writers describe how cold they are. In Text 1, the writer describes how 'The bedding was saturated and full of chill as the air was' while in Text 2, the writer describes all the clothes he wore in bed including 'two pairs of woolen socks on your feet and another on your hands, and a hat with earflaps tied beneath the chin' to show how cold it is in his bed.

supports the key point with evidence from Text 1

explains the significance of the evidence

1. Can you identify all the elements the student has included in this paragraph? Link ✏ the annotations to the paragraph to show where the student has included them.
2. Circle Ⓐ any adverbials that the student has used to signal comparison, for example:

both | also

Your turn!

You are now going to write your own answer in response to the exam-style question.

The two texts show the writers' experience of going to bed while staying at someone else's house.

What similarities do the writers' experiences share in these texts?

Use evidence from both texts to support your answer. **(6 marks)**

(1) Complete 🖉 the planning table below.

	1	2	3
Note down **three key similarities** you can write about in your response.			
For each similarity, choose a short, relevant **quotation** from each text.	Text 1	Text 1	Text 1
	Text 2	Text 2	Text 2
Look at each of your chosen quotations. Note down any **explanation** that you feel they need.	Text 1	Text 1	Text 1
	Text 2	Text 2	Text 2

(2) Use your notes to write 🖉 your response to the exam-style question above on paper.

Review your skills

Check up

Review your response to the exam-style question on page 55. Tick ⊘ the column to show how well you think you have done each of the following.

	Not quite ⊘	Nearly there ⊘	Got it! ⊘
identified key similarities	☐	☐	☐
supported points with relevant quotations from both texts	☐	☐	☐
explained the significance of evidence where needed	☐	☐	☐
structured an effective comparison using adverbials such as 'both', 'similarly', etc.	☐	☐	☐

Need more practice?

Here is another exam-style question, this time relating to Text 2, an extract from *The Battle of the Somme*, on page 74, and Text 3, an extract from *Going Commando* by Mark Time, on page 75. You'll find some suggested points to refer to in the Answers section.

Exam-style question

The two texts show the writers' experience of being a soldier.

What similarities do the writers' experiences share in these texts?

Use evidence from **both** texts to support your answer.

(6 marks)

How confident do you feel about each of these **skills?** Colour ✏ in the bars.

① How do I identify points of comparison?

② How do I synthesise information and ideas in two texts?

③ How do I write a comparison?

⑧ Comparing ideas and perpectives

This unit will help you learn how to compare the writers' ideas and perspectives in two different texts. The skills you will build are to:

* identify the writer's ideas and perspectives in each text
* explore ways to compare the two writers' ideas and perspectives
* structure an effective comparison.

In the exam you will face questions like the one below. This is about the texts on page 58. This unit will prepare you to write your own response to this question.

Exam-style question

Compare how the writers of text 1 and text 2 present their ideas and perspectives about animals.

Support your answer with detailed references to the texts.   **(14 marks)**

The three key questions in the **skills boosts** will help you compare the writers' ideas and perspectives.

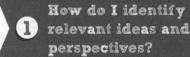
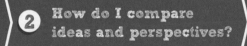
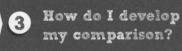

1 How do I identify relevant ideas and perspectives?

2 How do I compare ideas and perspectives?

3 How do I develop my comparison?

Read the two texts on page 58: an extract from *Never Cry Wolf* by Farley Mowat, published in 1963, and 'Pet Tales', a newspaper article published in 2012. You will tackle one 20th-century and one 21st-century non-fiction extract in the Reading section of your Paper 2 exam.

As you read, remember the following: ✓

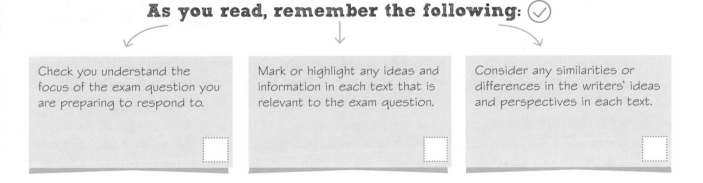

Check you understand the focus of the exam question you are preparing to respond to.

Mark or highlight any ideas and information in each text that is relevant to the exam question.

Consider any similarities or differences in the writers' ideas and perspectives in each text.

After several months observing a family of wolves in the Arctic Circle, naturalist Farley Mowat decided he needed to see the inside of their den (an underground burrow) while the wolves were out hunting.

Text 1 Never Cry Wolf, Farley Mowat

Reaching the entrance to the burrow I shed my heavy trousers, tunic and sweater, and taking a flashlight (whose batteries were very nearly dead) and measuring-tape from my pack, I began the difficult task of wiggling down the entrance tunnel.

5 The flashlight was so dim it cast only an orange glow – barely sufficient to enable me to read the marks on the measuring-tape. I squirmed onward, descending at a forty-five-degree angle, for about eight feet. My mouth and eyes were soon full of sand and I was beginning to suffer from claustrophobia, for the tunnel was just big enough to admit me.

At the eight-foot mark the tunnel took a sharp upward bend and swung to the left. I pointed the torch in the new direction and pressed the switch. Four green lights in the murk ahead reflected back the dim torch beam.

10 In this case green was not my signal to advance. I froze where I was, while my startled brain tried to digest the information that at least two wolves were with me in the den.

Despite my close familiarity with the wolf family, this was the kind of situation where irrational but deeply ingrained prejudices completely overmaster reason and experience. To be honest, I was so frightened that paralysis gripped me. I had no weapon of any sort, and in my awkward posture I could barely have gotten one
15 hand free with which to ward off an attack. It seemed inevitable that the wolves would attack me, for even a gopher will make a fierce defense when he is cornered in his den.

The wolves did not even growl.

Save for the two faintly glowing pairs of eyes, they might not have been there at all.

In this newspaper article, Poppy's owner writes about her life with his family.

Text 2 Pet Tales: Poppy, retired racing greyhound

We already knew Poppy had never set foot in a home when her adoption day came in 2009. Maybe we should have assumed that crossing the threshold signalled the start of another race for her: this time on an indoor track. Hurtling from room to room, leaping frantically at everything in sight – windows, worktops, televisions, and up the stairs (from which she was unable to fathom her way down). The whirlwind ended almost as quickly as it started
5 and from there on in, she transformed into the 45mph couch potato we were assured by the Retired Greyhound Trust she would become.

Her gentle, loving temperament became apparent as she settled in. It was luxury for her compared to kennel life. She adored lying full stretch in front of a warm radiator that winter; snoozing is her favourite pastime , in all manner of positions.
10

Poppy (or Abitachalk in the racing world) had a past we were eager to learn about. We investigated her ear tattoos, her family tree and found details of every race she ran (more than 100) and we were able to order a DVD of her racing.

We know she is thankful for a family and home life she could never have imagined in her racing years. She has rewarded us by becoming a much admired Pets As Therapy visiting dog, a valued Pet Blood Bank donor, and an appreciated Retired Greyhound Trust awareness dog, but most importantly, an adored family pet.

How do I identify relevant ideas and perspectives?

Before you can compare them, you need to identify the writer's ideas and perspectives in each text. To do this you need to think about:

- the writer, what they are writing about and why
- the ideas they include in the text and what these suggest about their attitudes and opinions.

1. The writer's perspective is the point of view from which they are writing. Read one student's notes on the writer's perspective in Text 2 on page 58, then look closely at Text 1 and complete their notes.

	Text 1	Text 2
What is the text about?		Adopting an ex-racing greyhound
Who is the writer?	A naturalist studying wolves	The dog's owner
Why are they writing it?		To show what great pets ex-racing greyhounds make

2. Track the writer's ideas through each text. What do they suggest about the writer's ideas and attitudes? Complete the notes below.

Text 1

A. He wriggles into the wolves' burrow.	This shows the writer is very dedicated to learning more about wolves.
B. He sees the wolves and panics.	This suggests ....
C. The wolves ignore him.	This gives the impression that ....

Text 2

A. Poppy had never been in a house when she was adopted.	This suggests that ex-racing greyhounds are ....
B. She ran around the house but soon settled down.	....
C. Her new family adore her.	....

3. Write one sentence summarising each writer's ideas and attitudes about animals.

The writer of Text 1 ....

....

The writer of Text 2 ....

....

Unit 8 Comparing ideas and perpectives 59

How do I compare ideas and perspectives?

When you compare texts, you need to look for ideas and perspectives that are:

- Similar, or
- linked in some way but very different.

① Look at one student's notes on the writer's ideas and perspectives in Text 1 on page 58.

> _Text 1_
>
> A. The writer is very dedicated to learning more about wolves.
>
> B. Wolves are wild animals and can be very dangerous.
>
> C. Wolves may not behave how you expect them to – they may be more scared of you than you are of them.

Now think about the ideas and perspectives suggested in Text 2 on page 58. Can you find a similarity or difference linked to the three key ideas in Text 1 above?

a Does Text 2 suggest that the writer is dedicated to his greyhound? Tick ✓ **one** answer.

| Yes, this is a similarity. | ☐ | No, this is a difference. | ☐ |

Write ✐ **one** sentence explaining how Text 2 is similar to or different from Text 1.

....

....

....

b Does Text 2 suggest that ex-racing greyhounds can be wild or dangerous? Tick ✓ **one** answer.

| Yes, this is a similarity. | ☐ | No, this is a difference. | ☐ |

Write ✐ **one** sentence explaining why.

....

....

....

c Does Text 2 suggest that ex-racing greyhounds behave unpredictably? Tick ✓ **one** answer.

| Yes, this is a similarity. | ☐ | No, this is a difference. | ☐ |

Write ✐ **one** sentence explaining why.

....

....

....

③ How do I develop my comparison?

When you compare the writers' ideas and perspectives in two texts, you need to comment on **how** the writers use **language and structure** to express those ideas and perspectives.

① Look at the sentences below, written by a student, comparing the writers' ideas and perspectives about animals in Text 1 and Text 2 on page 58

> In both texts the writers suggest that animals can be wild and unpredictable.

> For example, in Text 1, the writer bumps into two wolves in their den. He seems so sure that they will attack him, he is amazed that 'The wolves did not even growl.'

a Look at the quotation from Text 1 above. The writer uses simple language and a short simple sentence to express this idea. Write 🖉 sentences explaining why the writer might have made these choices.

....

....

....

b Now look at the start of the next sentence from the same student's response. Choose **one** quotation from Text 2 on page 58 to support this point and add 🖉 it to the response.

> Although the greyhound in Text 2 is not a dangerous animal, it is very wild and unpredictable when it first comes to its new owner's house. ....
>
> ....
>
> ....
>
> ....
>
> ....
>
> ....
>
> ....
>
> ....
>
> ....

c Look at your chosen quotation from Text 2 above. Circle Ⓐ any words or phrases in the quotation which suggest that the greyhound was wild and unpredictable when it first came to its new owner's house.

d What do these words or phrases suggest about the greyhound's behaviour? Add 🖉 **one or two** sentences to the response above, explaining your ideas.

Comparing ideas and perspectives

To write a good comparison of the writers' ideas and perspectives in two texts, you need to:

- identify each writer's ideas and perspectives
- identify significant similarities or differences in the writers' ideas and perspectives
- support each similarity or difference you identify with evidence from each text
- comment on how each writer uses language and/or structure to express their ideas and perspectives.

Now look at the exam-style question you saw at the start of the unit.

Exam-style question

Compare how the writers of text 1 and text 2 present their ideas and perspectives about animals.

Support your answer with detailed references to the texts. **(14 marks)**

Look at a paragraph written by one student in response to the exam-style question above.

identifies a key similarity in the two texts	compares the evidence from Text 1 with evidence from Text 2
supports the key similarity with evidence from Text 1	
explores the writer's use of language or structure in evidence from Text 1	explores the writer's use of language or structure in evidence from Text 2

Both writers are fascinated by the animals they are writing about. The writer of Text 1 goes to a lot of trouble to explore the wolves' den: 'I began the difficult task of wiggling down the entrance tunnel.' The word 'wiggling' shows how small and uncomfortable and difficult it was to get down there. Similarly, in Text 2, the writer goes to a lot of trouble to find out all about the greyhound's past life as a racing dog: 'We investigated her ear tattoos, her family tree and found details of every race she ran (more than 100) and we were able to order a DVD of her racing.' This long list shows how many things the dog's new owners did to find out more about their new pet.

1. Can you identify all the elements the student has included in this paragraph? Link 🖉 the annotations to the paragraph to show where the student has included them.

2. Circle Ⓐ any adverbials that the writer has used to signal comparison: for example,

both	also

Your turn!

You are now going to write your own answer in response to the exam-style question.

Compare how the writers of text 1 and text 2 present their ideas and perspectives about animals.

Support your answer with detailed references to the texts.   (14 marks)

① Complete ✐ the planning table below.

	1	2	3
Note down **three key similarities or differences** you can write about in your response.			
For each one, choose a relevant **quotation** from each text. Circle any key words or phrases you could comment on.	Text 1	Text 1	Text 1
	Text 2	Text 2	Text 2
Look at each of your chosen quotations. Note down comments you could make about the writer's use of language and/or structure.	Text 1	Text 1	Text 1
	Text 2	Text 2	Text 2

② Use your notes to write ✐ your response to the exam-style question above on paper.

Review your skills

Check up

Review your response to the exam-style question on page 63. Tick ✓ the column to show how well you think you have done each of the following.

	Not quite ✓	Nearly there ✓	Got it ✓
identified similarities and differences in the writers' ideas and perspectives	☐	☐	☐
supported my ideas with evidence from both texts	☐	☐	☐
commented on the writer's use of language and/or structure in each quotation	☐	☐	☐

Need more practice?

Below is another exam-style question, this time relating to Text 2, *The Battle of the Somme*, on page 74, and Text 3, an extract from *Going Commando* by Mark Time, on page 75. You'll find some suggested points to refer to in the Answers section.

Exam-style question

Compare how the writers of text 2 and text 3 present their ideas and perspectives about life as a soldier.

Support your answer with detailed references to the texts.

(14 marks)

How confident do you feel about each of these **skills?** Colour ✐ in the bars.

1 How do I identify relevant ideas and perspectives?

2 How do I compare ideas and perspectives?

3 How do I develop my comparison?

⑨ Expressing your ideas clearly and precisely

This unit will help you express your ideas clearly and precisely. The skills you will build are to:

- use appropriately formal, analytical language to express your ideas
- select vocabulary to express your ideas precisely
- select sentence structures to express your ideas clearly.

In the exam, you will face questions like the one below. This is about the text on page 66. This unit will prepare you to write your own response to this question.

Exam-style question

In this extract, there is an attempt to create a suspicious and untrustworthy character.

Evaluate how succesfully this is achieved.

Support your views with detailed reference to the text.

(15 marks)

The three key questions in the **skills boosts** will help you express your ideas clearly and precisely.

 ① How do I write a formal, analytical response?

 ② How do I express my ideas precisely?

 ③ How do I express my ideas clearly?

Read the extract on page 66 from *Oliver Twist* by Charles Dickens, first published in 1837. You will tackle a 19th-century fiction extract in the Reading section of your Paper 1 exam.

As you read, remember the following: ⊘

Check you understand the focus of the exam question you are preparing to respond to.

Mark or highlight any parts of the text relevant to the question you are going to answer: where the writer suggests that the boy that Oliver meets is suspicious or untrustworthy.

Oliver Twist is an orphan who has run away to London. He arrives in a town just outside London where he is approached by another boy.

Text 1 Oliver Twist, Charles Dickens

'Hullo, my covey! What's the row?'

The boy who addressed this inquiry to the young **wayfarer**, was about his own age: but one of the queerest looking boys that Oliver had ever seen. He was a snub-nosed, flat-browed, common-faced boy enough; and as dirty a juvenile as one would wish to see; but he had about him all the airs and manners of a man. He was short of

5   his age: with rather bow-legs, and little, sharp, ugly eyes. His hat was stuck on the top of his head so lightly, that it threatened to fall off every moment—and would have done so, very often, if the wearer had not had a knack of every now and then giving his head a sudden twitch, which brought it back to its old place again. He wore a man's coat, which reached nearly to his heels. He had turned the cuffs back, half-way up his arm, to get his hands out of the sleeves: apparently with the ultimate view of thrusting them into the pockets of his corduroy trousers; for

10   there he kept them. He was, altogether, as **roystering** and swaggering a young gentleman as ever stood four feet six, or something less, **in the bluchers**.

'Hullo, my covey! What's the row?' said this strange young gentleman to Oliver.

'I am very hungry and tired,' replied Oliver: the tears standing in his eyes as he spoke. 'I have walked a long way. I have been walking these seven days.'

15   'Walking for sivin days!' said the young gentleman. … 'You want grub, and you shall have it. I'm at low-water-mark myself—only **one bob and a magpie**; but, as far as it goes, I'll fork out and stump. Up with you on your pins. There! Now then! Morrice!'

Assisting Oliver to rise, the young gentleman took him to an adjacent chandler's shop, where he purchased a sufficiency of ready-dressed ham and a half-quartern loaf, or, as he himself expressed it, 'a fourpenny bran!', the

20   ham being kept clean and preserved from dust, by the ingenious expedient of making a hole in the loaf by pulling out a portion of the crumb, and stuffing it therein. Taking the bread under his arm, the young gentleman turned into a small public-house, and led the way to a tap-room in the rear of the premises. Here, a pot of beer was brought in, by direction of the mysterious youth; and Oliver, **falling to**, at his new friend's bidding, made a long and hearty meal, during the progress of which the strange boy eyed him from time to time with great attention.

25   'Going to London?' said the strange boy, when Oliver had at length concluded.

'Yes.'

'Got any lodgings?'

'No.'

'Money?'

30   'No.'

The strange boy whistled; and put his arms into his pockets, as far as the big coat-sleeves would let them go.

'Do you live in London?' inquired Oliver.

'Yes. I do, when I'm at home,' replied the boy. 'I suppose you want some place to sleep in to-night, don't you?'

'I do, indeed,' answered Oliver. 'I have not slept under a roof since I left the country.'

35   'Don't fret your eyelids on that score,' said the young gentleman. 'I've got to be in London to-night; and I know a **'spectable** old gentleman as lives there, wot'll give you lodgings for nothink….'

'Hullo, my covey! What's the row?': Hello mate, what's happening?
wayfarer: traveller
roystering: someone who enjoys themselves in a noisy, boisterous way
in the bluchers: in his boots
one bob and a magpie: a shilling and a halfpenny; coins of low value
falling to: tucking into the food
'spectable: respectable

How do I write a formal, analytical response?

The most successful responses are written in a formal, analytical style.

1 Look at the opening of one student's response, commenting on the presentation of a suspicious, untrustworthy character in the extract on page 66.

> The boy buys Oliver some food and drink and watches him closely: 'the strange boy eyed him from time to time with great attention'.

Look at all the words and phrases below which you could use to add to the above response.

	A.				B.	
☐	i.	This makes me think that		i.	a bit of a rogue	☐
☐	ii.	This means that		ii.	shady	☐
☐	iii.	This suggests that		iii.	dodgy	☐
☐	iv.	This creates the impression that	the boy is	iv.	dishonest	☐
☐	v.	This implies that		v.	cunning	☐
☐	vi.	This indicates that		vi.	devious	☐
☐	vii.	This tells me that		vii.	crafty	☐

a Which of the words and phrases above would you **not** use because they are **too informal**? Cross ⊗ them.

b Which of the words and phrases **might** you use because they are appropriate for a formal, analytical piece of writing? Tick ✎ them.

c Which of the words and phrases would **you** add to the above response? Choose **one** from column A and one from column B and circle Ⓐ them.

2 Look at another sentence from the student's response.

> The writer also says the boy is 'mysterious' which makes it sound like he's up to something pretty sneaky and isn't nice like he seems.

a Circle Ⓐ all the words and phrases that you feel could be more formal and/or analytical.

b Rewrite ✎ the comment, making it as formal and analytical as possible.

....

....

....

2 How do I express my ideas precisely?

When you write about a text, choose your vocabulary carefully to express your ideas as precisely as possible.

1 Look at a paragraph from one student's response, commenting on the presentation of a suspicious, untrustworthy character in the extract on page 66.

Choose one word to fill 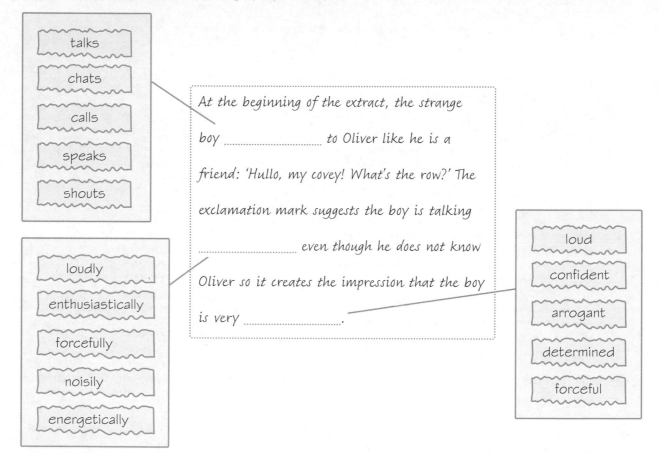 each gap. Choose the word that you feel:

- describes the text and the characters most accurately

- expresses the ideas in the paragraph precisely.

talks

chats

calls

speaks

shouts

loudly

enthusiastically

forcefully

noisily

energetically

At the beginning of the extract, the strange boy .... to Oliver like he is a friend: 'Hullo, my covey! What's the row?' The exclamation mark suggests the boy is talking .... even though he does not know Oliver so it creates the impression that the boy is very ....'

loud

confident

arrogant

determined

forceful

2 Now look at this comment about the strange boy who speaks to Oliver.

At first the boy appears to be nice because he buys Oliver some food and drink.

a Note down 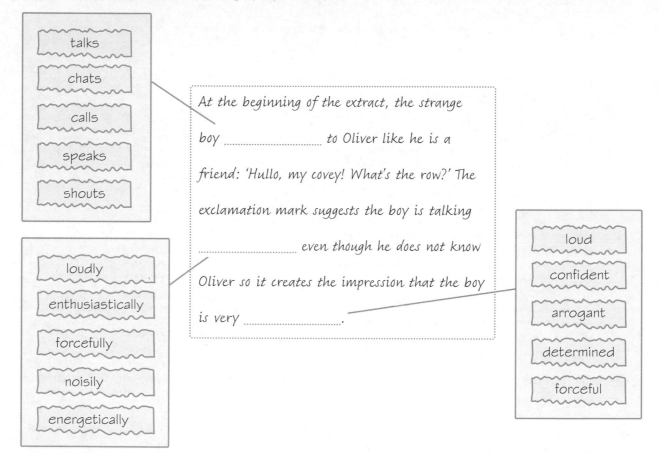 at least **three** words which could be used to describe the boy more precisely than the highlighted word.

A. .... ☐

B. .... ☐

C. .... ☐

b Which word describes the boy **most** precisely? Tick ✓ it.

③ How do I express my ideas clearly?

Short sentences can be used to express ideas simply. Linking **two or three** of those ideas **clearly and carefully** in a longer sentence can show how those ideas are related.

① Look at two students' ideas below, expressed in short sentences.

Rewrite their ideas, giving **two different versions** of each group of sentences, linking them to form a longer single sentence. In each version, experiment with:

- using different conjunctions (see word box for ideas) to link the ideas

and/or

- re-ordering the two or three ideas in the sentence.

> **Conjunctions**
>
> when   although
>
>   and
>
> because
>
>   but
>
> however
>
>   as

a
> Oliver is desperate for food and shelter. He has been walking for seven days. He has been sleeping in the open air.

Version 1 ....

.... ☐

Version 2 ....

.... ☐

b
> The strange boy seems kind and generous at first. He says he knows a man who will give Oliver lodgings for nothing. It seems more sinister and disturbing.

Version 1 ....

.... ☐

Version 2 ....

.... ☐

c Look at each pair of sentences you have written. Which one of each pair is more clearly expressed? Tick ✓ it.

② Look at another student's notes on the extract on page 66.

> he wore a man's coat, which nearly reached to his heels

> humourous eccentric character

> all the airs and manners of a man

> may not be as innocent as he first appears

> little, sharp, ugly eyes

> 'sharp' suggests devious and manipulative

Use the notes to write 🖉 **one or two** sentences in which all of the student's ideas are carefully linked using conjunctions.

....

....

....

....

Unit 9 Expressing your ideas clearly and precisely   69

Expressing your ideas clearly and precisely

To express your ideas clearly and precisely, you need to:

- express your ideas in a formal analytical style
- choose your vocabulary carefully to ensure you are expressing your ideas precisely
- use some shorter sentences to express your ideas clearly and simply
- use some longer sentences, linking ideas using carefully chosen conjunctions.

Now look at the exam-style question you saw at the start of the unit.

Exam-style question

In this extract, there is an attempt to create a suspicious and untrustworthy character.

Evaluate how succesfully this is achieved.

Support your views with detailed reference to the text.

(15 marks)

(1) Look at this paragraph from one student's response to the task.

> The strange boy has not got very much money but he still buys Oliver food and drink. This makes him seem nice, but perhaps too nice. Oliver is eating his bread and ham and drinking his beer and the writer says how the strange boy 'eyed him' all the time and this makes me think the boy is watching him sneakily and may be planning something and you begin to realise that Oliver may be in danger and not know.

a Is this paragraph written in a formal, analytical style? Circle (A) any words or phrases you feel could be improved. Note (✏) your suggested improvements in the margin.

b Could any of the vocabulary choices in the paragraph above be made more precise? Underline (A) any words or phrases you feel could be improved. Note (✏) your suggested improvements in the margin.

c One sentence in this paragraph is very long. How could you break it down into shorter sentences? How could you use a wider range of conjunctions to link some of the ideas and express them more clearly? Rewrite (✏) the sentence below.

....

....

....

....

....

....

Your turn!

You are now going to write your own answer in response to the exam-style question.

Exam-style question

In this extract, there is an attempt to create a suspicious and untrustworthy character.

Evaluate how succesfully this is achieved.

Support your views with detailed reference to the text.

(15 marks)

In your exam, you should spend around **20–25 minutes** on this type of question and write **four or five** paragraphs. However, you are now going to write just **one** paragraph. This will allow you to focus more closely on expressing your ideas as clearly and precisely as possible.

1 Look at some of the ways the writer tries to create a suspicious and untrustworthy character in the extract on page 66.

The strange boy's appearance	he had about him all the airs and manners of a man. ☐
	little, sharp, ugly eyes ☐
What the strange boy says	'Hullo, my covey! What's the row?' ☐
	'I know a 'spectable old gentleman as lives there, wot'll give you lodgings for nothink…' ☐
What the strange boy does	the strange boy eyed him from time to time with great attention. ☐
	a pot of beer was brought in, by direction of the mysterious youth ☐

a Choose **one** of the above which you can explore in your response to the exam-style question. Tick ✓ it.

b Use it to write ✐ a paragraph in response to the exam-style question. Remember to:

- write in a formal, analytical style

- choose your vocabulary carefully to express your ideas precisely

- think about how you structure your sentence to express your ideas clearly.

....

....

....

....

....

....

Review your skills

Check up

Review your response to the exam-style question on page 71. Tick ✓ the column to show how well you think you have done each of the following.

	Not quite ✓	Nearly there ✓	Got it! ✓
written in a formal, analytical style	☐	☐	☐
chosen vocabulary to express my ideas precisely	☐	☐	☐
chosen sentence structures to express my ideas clearly	☐	☐	☐

Need more practice?

You can EITHER:

① Look again at your paragraph written in response to the exam-style question on page 71. Rewrite ⟋ it, experimenting with different vocabulary choices and sentence structures, linking your ideas in different ways. Which are most effective in expressing your ideas clearly and precisely?

AND/OR

② Choose a **second** piece of advice from the suggestions on page 71. Write ⟋ a further paragraph in response to the exam-style question, focusing closely on your vocabulary choice and sentence structures.

How confident do you feel about each of these **skills?** Colour ⟋ in the bars.

① How do I write a formal, analytical response?

② How do I express my ideas precisely?

③ How do I express my ideas clearly?

More practice texts

An American travelling through France arrives in a village only to find that the village inn is full. The landlord of the inn offers him a room in a nearby house.

Text 1 The Cold Hand, Felix Octavius Carr Darley

Being quite **fatigued** with my day's ride, I desired to be shown to my sleeping room. It was of very moderate dimensions, and situated on the ground floor. In fact it was but barely large enough to afford room for a single bed, and a few inches of floor on one side of it where I might undress; and there was a window opening near the head of the bed.

5   I locked the door and undressed myself, threw my clothes upon the bed, and was soon fast asleep. I suppose I might have slept two hours, so that it was in the middle of night when I was suddenly awakened by a cold hand, as it might be the hand of a corpse, drawn deliberately over my face, from the forehead to the chin, and so passing off a space downward towards my feet! Horror-struck, I bolted upright, and I shouted in a tremulous but loud voice, "Who's there?" No answer. I stretched out my hands, and felt all the three walls of the room near the head

10   of the bed, and found nothing but the said bare walls. I then got upon my knees on the bed, and felt the walls all round the room, as I could easily do, by reason of its exceedingly limited dimensions. I then crept under the bed, and fully satisfied myself that there was no living creature in the room but myself.

It was mighty strange, I could have sworn that I had felt that awful cold hand passing over my face. The thing was done so coolly and deliberately, that there could be no mistake about it. Why did I not grasp the hand? you may

15   say. In fact I was waked out of **profound** sleep by its touch; and before I had time to seize it, it was gone. I stood wondering at the strange and incomprehensible nature of the thing for some minutes, and finally arrived at the reluctant admission that I must have been dreaming—that it was my imagination—that it was no hand at all, but the ghost of a hand.

In a very confused and unsettled state of mind, I at length got into bed again, and, still unrested from my fatigue,

20   I speedily fell into a doze. Before I had completely lost my consciousness, however, I felt the same appalling sensation as before—that horrible corpse-like hand dragging itself like the body of a serpent over my face. Horror of horrors! I screamed out at the utmost pitch of my voice, "Who's there? Who, what are you? Speak!"

I sprang instantly out of bed, and felt in the darkness all round the room again. There was no one to be found. There was nothing but empty space as before. I was completely dumb-founded. The former theory of dreams and

25   imaginations would not hold good now. The thing was too real. It was a hand, and nothing but a hand. I could swear to it. It might be, and probably was, the hand of a dead man; but it had skin and bones, and muscles and motion; and it had sent, I thought, all the blood in my body, back to my heart, as it passed over my face. It came and went this time more suddenly, so that I had not time to grasp at it, both of my hands being under the bed-clothes.

fatigued: tired, exhausted
profound: deep

In this extract the writer describes the events leading up to the death of his friend, Alan Seeger, at the Battle of the Somme in France in 1916. The battle was one of the deadliest of the First World War: it has been estimated that more than a million men were wounded or killed.

Text 2 The Battle of the Somme, Rif Baer

During the night of June 30–July 1 we left Bayonvillers to move nearer the firing line. We went to Proyart as reserves. At 8 o'clock on the morning of July 1st there was roll call for the day's orders and we were told that the general offensive would begin at 9 without us, as we were in reserve, and that we should be notified of the day and hour that we were to go into action. When this report was finished we were ordered to shell fatigue, unloading
5   8 inch shells from automobile trucks which brought them up to our position.

All was hustle and bustle. The **Colonial regiments** had carried the first German lines and thousands and thousands of prisoners kept arriving and leaving. Ambulances filed along the roads continuously. As news began to arrive we left our work to seek more details; everything we could learn seemed to **augur well**.

About 4 P. M. we left Proyart for Fontaine-les-Cappy and in the first line. Alan was beaming with joy and full of
10   impatience for the order to join the action. Everywhere delirious joy reigned at having driven the enemy back without loss for us. We believed that no further resistance would be met and that our shock attack would finish the Germans. After passing the night at Fontaine-les-Cappy we moved in the morning toward what had been the German first lines. I passed almost all the day with Alan. He was perfectly happy.

"My dream is coming true," he said to me, "and perhaps tomorrow we shall attack."

15   The field of battle was relatively calm, a few shells fell, fired by the enemy in retreat, and our troops were advancing on all sides. The Colonials had taken Assevillers and the next day we were to take their place in first line. On July 3rd about noon we moved toward Assevillers to relieve the Colonials at nightfall. Alan and I visited Assevillers, the next morning, picking up souvenirs, postcards, letters, soldiers' notebooks, and chatting all the time, when suddenly a voice called out: "The company will fall in to go to the first line."

20   About 4 o'clock the order came to get ready for the attack. None could help thinking of what the next few hours would bring. One minute's anguish and then, once in the ranks, faces became calm and serene, a kind of gravity falling upon them, while on each could be read the determination and expectation of victory. Two battalions were to attack Belloy-en-Santerre, our company being the reserve of battalion. The companies forming the first wave were deployed on the plain. Bayonets glittered in the air above the corn, already quite tall.

25   The first section (Alan's section) formed the right and vanguard of the company and mine formed the left wing. After the first bound forward, we lay flat on the ground, and I saw the first section advancing beyond us and making toward the extreme right of the village of Belloy-en-Santerre. I caught sight of Seeger and called to him, making a sign with my hand.

He answered with a smile. How pale he was! His tall silhouette stood out on the green of the cornfield. He was the
30   tallest man in his section. His head erect, and pride in his eye, I saw him running forward, with bayonet fixed. Soon he disappeared and that was the last time I saw my friend. . .

colonial regiments: regiments fighting with the allied forces of Britain, France and the USA
augur well: suggest that the battle was going well

At the age of 16, Mark Time decided he wanted to become a Royal Marine Commando. In this extract, he begins his basic training.

Text 3 Going Commando, Mark Time, 2015

Despite it being near-freezing, the PTI wore only a snow-white vest on his top half. 'Keep moving, fellas,' he yelled, before barking out instructions at high speed. 'No one stands still on the bottom field! Five-second sprint GO! Ten press-ups, ten sit-ups, ten star-jumps, GO! Roll over, roll over, roll over, ten sit-ups, GO! Roll over, roll over, roll over that wall, GO! Back again, not quick enough! Front support position place! That's press-ups to you, fellas. Arms
5 bend and stretch arms, bend and stretch. Ten star-jumps, GO! Hurry up! Not quick enough, that wall, GO!'

And so it continued, a white noise of incomprehensible, ungrammatical shouting that confused us to the point of doing everything wrong. Some of us were doing press-ups while others were rolling into those who were still doing sit-ups, or tripping up people who were sprinting like headless chickens in no discernible direction.

Knackered by the warm-up, we moved on to the height confidence test. Before us stood a large steel structure
10 with thin wooden planks spanning its length. Not ever having been higher than the climbing frame at primary school, I really didn't know how I'd cope at 7m up. As I stood at the bottom of the ladder ready to climb, I hoped my legs didn't turn to jelly like the lad in front of me.

'Come on you, don't take all day,' shouted the PTI – I hoped at someone else.

'I can't do it, Corporal,' the guy above me shouted.

15 'Can't or won't?' the PTI shouted back.

I don't think he was in a position to respond to such a rhetorical question. He just stood transfixed on the ladder, his knuckles white from his vice-like grip.

'Right, get down. Hurry up!'

The lad slowly made his way down the ladder. He was sent over to the PRC corporal and sat down. I doubted he
20 would become a Royal Marine – or a window cleaner, for that matter.

It did nothing for my own confidence, but once I was up there I felt okay, despite having only a narrow plank of bendy wood between me and **quadriplegia**.

Although I'd thought myself pretty fit – playing sport almost continuously and being able to outrun the police – I'd never felt the pain of cramp. Running up the hill towards the metal gate on the assault course, I felt it for
25 the first time. I managed to finish, wincing with pain, and veered towards a PTI who laughingly pulled me to the floor. He stretched my calves to ease the pain and sent me on my way to warm down. I thought I'd blown my chance. Needing immediate attention after completing the assault course surely meant I wasn't fit enough to pass?

quadriplegia: paralysis of the arms and legs, caused by injury or illness

Answers

Unit 1

Page 3

① KEY: B; DETAIL: A, C, E; X: D

② ⓐ For example:

Paragraph 2: The McDonald brothers were unhappy with the drive-in business and decided to try something new.

Paragraph 3: The brothers changed every aspect of the way they ran their restaurant.

Paragraph 4: McDonald's soon became very popular.

Page 4

① **inform** (for example, paragraph 1 informs the reader about the McDonald brothers' career); **explain** (for example, paragraph 2 explains why the brothers were dissatisfied with their drive-in restaurant)

② ⓐ ⓑ

A. Early failures suggest that their later success may have involved some luck.

B. The invention of the Speedee Service System suggests their business skill.

C. The changes they implemented, notably firing all their carhops, suggests ruthlessness.

Page 5

① ⓐ D is the most relevant, detailed and accurate summary of the extract.

ⓑ For example, combining some elements of the summaries and adding further key information: The McDonald brothers were clever businessmen who transformed their successful drive-in restaurant by inventing the way that fast food is made and sold.

② The information in the opening paragraph suggests that the McDonald brothers were lucky to succeed with their restaurant business. By the end of the text, we are left with the impression that they were bold and innovative businessmen.

Page 6

① Question **1** and question **2/1** are correct.

② Question **2/2** does not answer the question. It summarises the extent of the changes made but is not an example suggesting how much it changed. More accurate answers might include, for example, getting rid of dishes and glassware, replacing cooks with the principles of a factory assembly line, etc.

Page 7

For example:

① They bought a mansion with a tennis court and a pool.

② 1 They were tired of constantly looking for new staff.

2 They did not like their mainly teenage customers or their behaviour.

Page 8

• They are in reserve.

• Thousands of prisoners arrive and leave; ambulances file along the roads continuously.

Unit 2

Page 11

① All are arguable.

Page 12

① ⓐ For example: 'scarlet blot'; 'a gigantic ace of hearts'

② ⓐ For example: 'Mrs Brooks had strange qualms of misgiving'; 'she could not bring herself to attempt the handle.'

Page 13

① A. More effective

B. Most effective

C. Least effective

② For example:
The writer describes the sound of blood dripping from the murdered man: 'Drip, drip, drip.' Repeating the word 'drip' helps you imagine the scary sound of the blood dripping and hitting the floor with a regular beat and the short sentence adds to the tension and drama.

Page 14

①

Identifies a relevant idea from the text	The writer describes how Mrs Brooks tries to work out what the stain on the ceiling is
Supports key idea with a quotation from the text	'touched the spot in the ceiling with her fingers. It was damp'
Comments on the effect of the writer's choices	it makes you think of her getting the blood on her hands which is disgusting especially when the writer says that 'It was damp'
Comments on the impact of the writer's choices on the reader	She works it out quite slowly so it helps to make this part of the story really dramatic and tense.

② For example:
The writer describes how Mrs Brooks tries to work out what the stain on the ceiling is: ~~'touched the spot in the ceiling with her fingers. It was damp'. This shows she is trying to work out what the stain is.~~ The writer says she touched it 'with her fingers' which is obvious but it makes you think of her getting the blood on her hands which is disgusting especially when the

writer says that 'It was damp'. She works it out quite slowly so it helps to make this part of the story really dramatic and tense.

Page 16

Language
- The writer is 'confused and unsettled'
- Use of adjectives, e.g. 'appalling', 'horrible'
- Unpleasant image of the cold hand compared to 'the body of a serpent' being dragged across his face

Structure
- Contrast of peace and rest with sudden terrors at the touch of the cold hand
- Short emphatic exclamation of 'Horror of horrors!'
- Short sentences, e.g. 'The thing was too real. It was a hand, and nothing but a hand. I could swear to it', suggest racing thoughts and rising tension.

Unit 3

Page 19

(1) (a) H is not featured in the extract.

(b) A, B and C are the focus of the extract.

Page 20

(1) (a) Both are arguable. 'Likes expensive things' is, perhaps, more apparent in this section of the text.

(b)(c)(d) For example: 'his oxidized gold cigarette case' and 'best quality folio typing paper' suggest Fleming's expensive tastes.

(2) For example: 'rattled the story down'; 'swift assurance'; '2,000 words a day'

Page 21

(1) (a) All are arguable, although the suggestion that 'Bond is a baby' would need further explanation!

(b) All are arguable.

(2) For example: 'rattled' suggests the sound of the typewriter and the pace at which Fleming wrote the novel, adding to the impression that he wrote the novel 'effortlessly'.

Page 22

Uses key words from the question	One way the writer interests the reader
Identifies a key idea in the text	is by showing what Ian Fleming was like.
Explains the impression created	The writer creates the impression that Fleming had a strict routine when he wrote his stories.
Identifies a word or phrase that creates that impression	The writer explains that Fleming would write his story 'Every morning between nine and twelve'. The phrase 'every morning'
Comments on what the word or phrase suggests	suggests he did the same thing every day
Comments on what the word or phrase makes the reader think or feel	which makes me think he was a very organised and determined person.

Page 24

Language
- Use of humorous comparisons, e.g. 'Not ever having been higher than the climbing frame at primary school'
- Vivid description of the other trainee's fear: 'transfixed on the ladder, his knuckles white from his vice-like grip'
- Description of the structure the writer has to climb suggests its size and instability: 'a large steel structure… a narrow plank of bendy wood between me and quadriplegia'

Structure
- PTI speaks in short exclamations and writer uses frequent capital letters to suggest he is barking a very fast sequence of demanding instructions
- Rhetorical question at the end of the extract engages the reader's interest

Unit 4

Page 27

(1) For example: The writer aims to shock the reader and encourage their sympathy for the families living in the camp.

(2) (a) travel: the writer approaches and moves through the camp
contrast: the writer contrasts one family's life before the Depression with their life in camp
narrowing focus: the writer approaches the camp, focuses on one house, then focuses on the family that lives there

(b) The use of travel and narrowing focus creates the impression that the reader is with the writer as he walks through and records his observations.

The use of contrast encourages the reader's sympathy.

Page 28

(1) (a) For example:

C, E: They raised chickens, pigs, pigeons and vegetables and fruit for their own use; and their land produced the tall corn of the middle west.

A, E: Now they have nothing.

D: But one night he went into convulsions and died, and the next morning the coroner's wagon took him away.

B: It was one step down.

(b) For example: The first, short sentence is a dramatic statement, highlighting the dirt and degradation of life in the camp. The second, longer sentence adds a series of details which build to develop this impression.

Page 29

(1) (a) All are valid.

(b) All are valid.

(2) This short, blunt sentence dramatically emphasises the poverty of this family, particularly in contrast to the longer sentence before it, listing all that they used to have. It helps to add to the reader's sympathy for them.

Page 30

uses key words from the question	The writer engages and interests the reader
explains the impression created	by making the reader feel sorry for the people living in the camp.
uses evidence to support the impression created	At the start of the text he describes the camp. He says 'From a distance it looks like a city dump.' Then he focuses in on one house and the people who have to live there in a house made of corrugated paper.
comments on the impact of the writer's choice of structure	This means you feel like you are with the writer walking up to the camp and then looking at the houses and then the people.
comments on what the writer's choice of structure makes the reader think or feel	It makes you sympathise with the people in the camp because you see the way they have to live.

Page 32

Language
- Description of Seeger's happiness: 'perfectly happy'… "My dream is coming true."
- Positive description of weapons suggests the soldiers have no idea of the horrors of battle: 'Bayonets glittered in the air'
- Description suggests soldiers' mixed emotions once called to the first line: 'anguish', 'calm', 'serene'.

Structure
- Contrast between the soldiers' happiness at joining the battle, their hopes of victory, and the tragic outcome
- Listing of how the soldiers occupy themselves suggests a range of everyday activities: 'picking up souvenirs, postcards, letters, soldiers' notebooks, and chatting all the time'
- These activities sharply contrasted with the order to join the battle: 'suddenly a voice called out: "The company will fall in to go to the first line."'

Unit 5

Page 35

1.
   a. C
   b. B
   c. A
   d. e. All three comments are effective; however, comment A is arguably the most effective as it combines comment on language and structure.

2.
   a. For example: The writer lists all the things he was doing in the sky in this longer sentence. He is 'soaring and swooping' and 'skimming' and 'hopping'. This makes it sound like he is moving fast and he is in control.
   b. For example: The word 'world' shows the extreme violence of the impact with which he hit the ground and its effect on him.

Page 36

1.
   a. A
   b. A
   c. B
   d. C

2./3. All are valid choices.

Page 37

1.
   a. A, B
   b. D, F, G
   c. E
   d. A, C, E, F are relevant and valid. B is not relevant to the focus on paramotoring being exciting. D does not focus on a specific language choice and is not relevant to the focus.
   e. For example: A, C, E, F

Page 38

uses key words from the question	The writer engages the reader
identifies a significant impression created in the text	by building up the tension as he describes falling to the ground:
identifies a significant sentence structure	Using short sentences
comments on how sentence structure adds to the impression created	makes it sound like it is happening very quickly and like he is panicking… the short sentence makes you realise how everything stopped when he hit it.
identifies a significant language choice	The last one of these short sentences is just one word 'Wallop.'
comments on how language choice adds to the impression created	This word makes you realise how hard he hit the ground

Page 40

Language
- The narrator is 'horror-struck', suggesting his terror.
- The narrator 'bolted' upright, suggesting sudden, frightened movement.
- His voice is 'tremulous'.

Structure
- A sudden contrast of mood moves from the peace of sleep to sheer terror.
- Lengthy sentence describing the hand drawn from his face down towards his feet suggests a long moment of terror.
- The writer builds tension with short sentences: '"Who's there?" No answer.'

Unit 6

Page 43

1. All are used to create a sense of danger.

2. B, C

3. A, C

4. For example: The writer builds a sense of danger by describing Dracula's strange appearance, the narrator's thoughts and feelings about Dracula, and the strange things that Dracula says.

Page 44

1 shudder; rank; horrible feeling of nausea

2 The comments on the left focus on what the writer has done; those on the right focus on how this helps the writer achieve his intention.

1 **a** the howling of many wolves; gleamed; the children of the night; music

b Describing wolves as 'children' and their howling as 'music' suggests Dracula does not fear them and that he may be more like a wolf than a human.

Page 45

1 **a** All are valid.

Page 46

identifies where the writer has tried to achieve their intention	The narrator describes Count Dracula in a lot of detail. One of the most strange and frightening details is his nails: 'The nails were long and fine, and cut to a sharp point.'
comments on what the writer has done	Because they are 'cut to a sharp point',
comments on how what the writer has done helps the writer's intention	it makes you think he has nails that are a bit like claws and it makes you think of Dracula's sharp teeth and the wolves that are heard at the end of the extract.
comments on the success of its impact on the reader	This really builds up the sense of danger because it feels like the narrator is sitting with a wild animal who could attack him at any minute.

Page 48

- The description of the cold hand conveys a frightening experience when compared to 'the hand of a corpse' and 'the body of a serpent'.
- The repeated waking, feeling the hand, searching, and finding nothing, creates a sense of mystery and suggests the supernatural is at work.
- Use of speech suggests the narrator's terror.

Unit 7

Page 51

1 **a** Text 1: All are relevant.

Text 2: A, B and C are not relevant.

b For example:
   E. He squashes the bed bugs. They smell and are full of the writer's blood.
   F. The writer also finds fleas and lice.
   G. The writer gets dressed to protect himself and gets back into bed.
   All are relevant.

c For example:
   F. The writer puts on layers and layers of clothing to try to keep warm.
   G. The writer then has lots and lots of blankets, coats and a carpet put on him. It's like 'sleeping under a dead horse'.
   H. At first it is freezing but he soon warms up.
   All are relevant.

Page 52

1 For example:
- temperature
- mattress
- discomfort
- clothing

2 For example:

a Both writers describe an uncomfortable mattress.

b Both writers complain of cold and discomfort.

Page 53

1 **a** For example:

Text 1: 'I put on my coat, buttoned my pants outside it, put my socks on, got into bed, turned out the lamp, turned up my coat collar, wrapped my head in my shirt, stuck my hands under my coat at the chest, and tried to go to sleep.'

Text 2: 'First, you put on long underwear, pajamas, jeans, a sweatshirt, your grandfather's old cardigan and bathrobe, two pairs of woolen socks on your feet and another on your hands, and a hat with earflaps tied beneath the chin.'

b For example:

In Text 1, the writer describes how he 'put on my coat, buttoned my pants outside it' and 'wrapped my head in my shirt'.

In a similar way, the writer of Text 2 explains how he had to put on 'long underwear, pajamas, jeans' and 'two pairs of woolen socks on your feet and another on your hands'.

c The writer of Text 1 does this to try to stop the bedbugs, lice and fleas biting him.

This is because the writer of Text 2 is trying to keep warm in a very cold room.

Page 54

1

identifies a key similarity in the two texts	In both texts, the writers describe how cold they are.
supports the key point with evidence from Text 1	In Text 1, the writer describes how 'The bedding was saturated and full of chill as the air was'
supports the key point with evidence from Text 2	while in Text 2, the writer describes all the clothes he wore in bed including 'two pairs of woolen socks on your feet and another on your hands, and a hat with earflaps tied beneath the chin'
explains the significance of the evidence	to show how cold it is in his bed.

2 both, while

Page 56

- Both texts show that soldiers must obey orders.
- Both texts show that soldiers must be brave and determined.
- Both texts show that being a soldier is difficult and challenging.

Unit 8

Page 59

(1) What is the text about? Exploring a wolves' den.

Why are they writing it? It is a surprising story about how wolves behave.

(2) Text 1

B. This suggests he is in a very dangerous situation.

C. This gives the impression that wolves are not as dangerous as we might think.

Text 2

A. This suggests that racing greyhounds do not have very comfortable lives.

B. This shows that ex-racing greyhounds can be nervous and unpredictable.

C. This gives the impression that adopting an ex-racing greyhound can be very rewarding.

(3) The writer of Text 1 cannot help being frightened when he is trapped with wolves, but they seem to be even more frightened of him.

The writer of Text 2 shows how adopting a greyhound can be difficult at first but very rewarding in the end.

Page 60

(1) **a** Yes, the writer is very dedicated to his greyhound. He finds out all about her past and says she is an 'adored family pet'.

b Yes, ex-racing greyhounds can be wild. When she first arrives, Poppy hurtles around the house.

c No, ex-racing greyhounds are more predictable. The writer was told that Poppy would soon settle down and she does.

Page 61

(1) **a** The simple language and short, simple sentence structure add emphasis to this point, highlighting the writer's surprise.

b For example: 'Hurtling from room to room, leaping frantically at everything in sight – windows, worktops, televisions'

c **d** The word 'hurtling' suggests the greyhound's speed and the phrase 'leaping frantically' shows how anxious and desperate she was. The list of things she leaps at emphasise how frantic and wild she was.

Page 62

identifies a key similarity in the two texts	Both writers are fascinated by the animals they are writing about.
supports the key similarity with evidence from Text 1	The writer of Text 1 goes to a lot of trouble to explore the wolves' den: 'I began the difficult task of wiggling down the entrance tunnel.'
explores the writer's use of language or structure in evidence from Text 1	The word 'wiggling' shows how small and uncomfortable and difficult it was to get down there.
compares the evidence in Text 1 with evidence from Text 2	Similarly, in Text 2, the writer goes to a lot of trouble to find out all about the greyhound's past life as a racing dog: 'We investigated her ear tattoos, her family tree and found details of every race she ran (more than 100) and we were able to order a DVD of her racing.'
explores the writer's use of language or structure in evidence from Text 2	This long list shows how many things the dog's new owners did to find out more about their new pet.

(2) Both, Similarly

Page 64

- Both texts show the difficulties of life as a soldier. Text 2 suggests the pain of losing a friend: 'that was the last time I saw my friend…'; Text 3 vividly describes the pain of completing an assault course: 'wincing with pain'.

- Text 3 clearly shows the role of senior officers and their relationship with the soldiers: "Ten star-jumps, GO! Hurry up! Not quick enough, that wall, GO!"; in Text 2, there is very little reference to officers, only the receiving of orders.

- Text 2 is surprisingly positive: 'expectation of victory'; Text 3 expects failure: 'Needing immediate attention after completing the assault course surely meant I wasn't fit enough to pass?'

Unit 9

Page 67

1 **a** In column A, all are appropriately formal. In column B, i, ii, iii, and viii, are inappropriately informal.

b In column A, iii, iv, v, vi and viii are more appropriate for a formal analytical response. In column B, iv, v, vi and viii are more appropriate for a formal analytical response.

2 **a** For example: says, makes it sound, up to something pretty sneaky, isn't nice like

b For example: The writer describes the boy as 'mysterious', which suggests that he may be attempting to manipulate Oliver and is not as generous and kind as he seems.

Page 68

1 All are acceptable; however, the most precise, accurate choices are arguably:
- talks, calls, speaks
- enthusiastically, forcefully, energetically
- confident, forceful.

2 **a** For example: generous, helpful, friendly, thoughtful, considerate, kind

Page 69

1 **a** For example:
- Oliver is desperate for food and shelter <u>because</u> he has been walking for seven days <u>and</u> has been sleeping in the open air.
- <u>Because</u> he has been walking for seven days <u>and</u> has been sleeping in the open air, Oliver is desperate for food and shelter.

b For example:
- The strange boy seems kind and generous at first <u>but when</u> he says he knows a man who will give Oliver lodgings for nothing, <u>it</u> seems more sinister and disturbing.
- <u>Although</u> the strange boy seems kind and generous at first, <u>it</u> seems more sinister and disturbing when he says he knows a man who will give Oliver lodgings for nothing.

2 He is presented as a humorous, eccentric character but it is suggested that he may be devious and manipulative and not as innocent as he first appears.

Page 70

1 For example: The strange boy has not got very much money but he still buys Oliver food and drink. This ~~makes him seem~~ creates the impression that he is ~~nice~~ generous, but perhaps too ~~nice~~ generous. When Oliver is eating his bread and ham and drinking his beer, and the writer ~~says~~ describes how the strange boy 'eyed him' all the time. ~~and~~ This ~~makes me think~~ suggests the boy is watching him ~~sneakily~~ surreptitiously and may be planning something. ~~and~~ You begin to realise that Oliver may be in danger ~~and~~ yet not ~~know~~ be aware of it.